A beautiful book packed wit
Beloved and Blessed covers eve
of the marital relationship, to t.. basics of kids' budgeting, to coping
with trials and tragic loss. A welcome addition to the *Life-Nurturing
Love* series which keeps getting better and better.

—Karen Edmisten, author, *The Rosary:
Keeping Company With Jesus and Mary*

When you read Kimberly Hahn you can't help but feel you are receiving the best advice from a wise and cherished friend. With good
humor and joy, Kimberly offers Christ-centered teaching from the
heart of the Church in her unique maternal-nurturing way. *Beloved
and Blessed* is one of the most important witnesses in recent times on
how to truly live out God's design for marriage.

—Kris McGregor, Spirit Catholic Radio,
Morning Show cohost and producer

I heartily recommend *Beloved and Blessed* to women (men too!) who
are trying to confront, in a fruitful and faithful way, the many challenges to Christian family life today. At once biblical and highly personal, it is filled with lively anecdotes and combines a firm knowledge
of Christian tradition with sound common sense and lots of loving,
hard-won experience.

—Evelyn Birge Vitz, author, *A Continual Feast:
A Cookbook to Celebrate the Joys of Family
and Faith Throughout the Christian Year*

Kimberly Hahn opens the door to her own home and invites us in.
She draws from Proverbs 31 and her wisdom from the trenches to tenderly and honestly discuss intimacy, nurturing affection with our
spouse, finances, education, sharing family faith, and disciplining our
children in the heart of the Catholic home. *Beloved and Blessed* will
enrich your understanding of married and family life and you'll be very
glad you stopped in for the visit.

—Donna-Marie Cooper O'Boyle, author,
The Domestic Church: Room by Room

This comprehensive guide for marital relations, homemaking, family life, and parenting is written in a winsome, fresh, understandable, and practical style. Kimberly Hahn keeps the book personal as she shares her own struggles and successes. The discussion on fertility in light of eternity is worth the price of the book several times over. In a world where confusion abounds regarding marriage, family life, sexuality, and the goodness of children, *Beloved and Blessed* is a reliable and faithful witness to the truth. I urge every family to obtain a copy.

—Steve Wood, president, Family Life Center International

In our book, *Raising Money-Smart Kids,* my wife and I outlined a system of teaching money management that we used with our five children. Kimberly Hahn has taken it to a new level. As I read her chapter about how she and her husband trained their children to manage money, I was so encouraged to see a great refinement on the process that my wife and I taught in our original book. I would recommend *Beloved and Blessed* for that chapter alone, but as I reviewed the manuscript I saw such a wealth of marriage and parenting principles that I can recommend it whole-heartedly to all who are seeking a godly marriage and family.

—Ronald W. Blue, president, Kingdom Advisors

BELOVED AND BLESSED

BELOVED
AND
BLESSED

BIBLICAL
WISDOM
FOR
FAMILY
LIFE

Kimberly Hahn

PUBLISHED BY ST. ANTHONY MESSENGER PRESS
CINCINNATI, OHIO

RESCRIPT

In accord with the *Code of Canon Law*, I hereby grant my permission to publish *Beloved and Blessed: Biblical Wisdom for Family Life*.

Most Reverend R. Daniel Conlon
Bishop
Diocese of Steubenville
Steubenville, Ohio
October 19, 2009

The permission to publish is a declaration that a book or pamphlet is considered to be free of doctrinal or moral error. It is not implied that those who have granted the permission to publish agree with the contents, opinions or statements expressed.

Unless otherwise noted, Scripture passages have been taken from the *Revised Standard Version*, Catholic edition. Copyright 1946, 1952, 1971 by the Division of Christian Education of the National Council of Churches of Christ in the USA. Used by permission. All rights reserved. Scripture passages marked *NAB* are from the *New American Bible With Revised New Testament and Psalms*. Copyright ©1991, 1986, 1970 by the Confraternity of Christian Doctrine, Inc., Washington, D.C. Used with permission. All rights reserved.

Note: The editors of this volume have made minor changes in capitalization to some of the Scripture quotations herein. Please consult the original source for proper capitalization.

Quotes are taken from the English translation of the *Catechism of the Catholic Church* for the United States of America (indicated as *CCC*), 2nd ed. Copyright 1997 by United States Catholic Conference—Libreria Editrice Vaticana.

Cover and book production by Mark Sullivan
Cover image: Agnolo Bronzino, The Holy Family
Photo credit: Alinari / Art Resource, NY

LIBRARY OF CONGRESS CATALOGING-IN-PUBLICATION DATA
Hahn, Kimberly.
  Beloved and blessed : Biblical wisdom for family life / Kimberly Hahn.
      p. cm.
  Includes bibliographical references (p.   ) and index.
  ISBN 978-0-86716-945-4 (pbk. : alk. paper) 1. Families—Religious life. 2. Families—Biblical teaching. 3. Catholic Church—Doctrines. I. Title.
  BX2351.H33 2010
  248.8'45—dc22
                                        2009047162
ISBN 978-0-86716-945-4

Published by Servant Books, an imprint of St. Anthony Messenger Press.
28 W. Liberty St.
Cincinnati, OH 45202
www.ServantBooks.org

Printed in the United States of America.

Printed on acid-free paper.

10 11 12 13 14 5 4 3 2 1

To Hannah, my daughter—for the joy of sharing life with another girl all of these years, and for your love for each member of our family

To Sarah, my first daughter-by-covenant—for the gift you are to each of us, and especially for the ways you love my son, Gabriel, my first granddaughter, Veronica Margaret, and the little one on the way

To Ana, my second daughter-by-covenant—for the gift you are to each of us, and especially for the ways you love my son, Michael, and my second granddaughter, Naomi Therese

Special thanks to Kathy McQuaig for her editorial help, to Julieta Robbins for her words of encouragement and delicious meals so I could write, and to Pat Decker for her help with the manuscript, along with other dear friends who have prayed for me throughout this project.

Contents

INTRODUCTION   xiii

PART ONE
The Heart of Her Husband Trusts in Her   1

CHAPTER ONE
Invitation to Intimacy   3

CHAPTER TWO
Challenges to Intimacy   15

PART TWO
Her Children Rise Up and Call Her Blessed   33

CHAPTER THREE
Family as the Sanctuary of Life   35

CHAPTER FOUR
The Mission of Responsible Parenthood   47

CHAPTER FIVE
Answering the Critics   56

CHAPTER SIX
Training Our Hearts in Truth   66

PART THREE
She Makes Linen Garments and Sells Them   77

CHAPTER SEVEN
Facing the Financial Future Without Fear   79

CHAPTER EIGHT
Economics of a Stay-at-Home Mom   94

CHAPTER NINE
Mary, Model for Mothers   103

PART FOUR
Her Husband Is Known in the Gates   111

CHAPTER TEN
The Perfect Parent   113

CHAPTER ELEVEN
*Bringing Up Children With Discipline
and Instruction*   130

PART FIVE
She Opens Her Mouth With Wisdom   143

CHAPTER TWELVE
Making a Home for the Word   145

CHAPTER THIRTEEN
Living Witness: Sharing the Faith in Our Family   159

PART SIX
The Teaching of Kindness Is on Her Tongue   171

CHAPTER FOURTEEN
Sculpting a Life Through Education at Home   173

CHAPTER FIFTEEN
Training in Practical Life Skills   185

CHAPTER SIXTEEN
Trusting God When Parenting Hurts   200

APPENDIX A
Video Outlines   215

APPENDIX B
Questions for an Intergenerational Women's Study   227

APPENDIX C
Family Budget Items   231

APPENDIX D
Kids' Budgets   234

APPENDIX E
Stewardship of the Home   235

APPENDIX F
The Power of the Tongue   237

RECOMMENDED RESOURCES   238

NOTES   244

Introduction

Welcome to the third installment of the *Life-Nurturing Love* series! Before we begin, allow me to offer a quick overview.

Proverbs 31 records the instructions of a queen mother to her son, King Lemuel, so that she can guide him as he selects a wife. She wants him to understand the characteristics of a godly woman, who can make the difference not only in his life but also in the well-being of the kingdom. Her instructions help other men consider carefully who they will marry, and they help women discern attributes to cultivate in their lives.

We are treating Proverbs 31 in a way similar to a table of contents, so that we can look at a variety of Scriptures that address these characteristics and how they can be developed. In the first series of six studies, *Chosen and Cherished: Biblical Wisdom for Your Marriage*, we studied Proverbs 31:10-12:

> Who can find a good wife?
>> She is far more precious than jewels.
> The heart of her husband trusts in her,
>> and he will have no lack of gain.
> She does him good, and not harm,
>> all the days of her life.

A good wife is a godly wife, one who loves the Lord. She understands her sense of worth based on the Lord who made her and who redeems her. Through her godly fear of the Lord, her highest priorities are to love and serve the Lord through her vocation. Her love for the Lord enables her to love her neighbor (spouse and children) as she loves herself.

We focused on marriage as the core relationship of the family and how we can build a healthy marriage on the foundation of trust, mutual respect, and love. We examined how to appreciate the complementarity of the husband as the head of the home and the wife as the heart of home in the delicate dance of loving service. We also reviewed the wedding vow, phrase by phrase, and how we can be faithful to it. Finally we studied Jesus' teaching on divorce and the indissolubility of marriage.

In the second series of six studies, *Graced and Gifted: Biblical Wisdom for the Homemaker's Heart,* we considered how relationships are key to homemaking. Our tasks flow from our love, so that priority loving leads to priority living. We studied Proverbs 31:13-17:

> She seeks wool and flax,
> and works with willing hands.
> She is like the ships of the merchant,
> she brings her food from afar.
> She rises while it is yet night
> and provides food for her household
> and tasks for her maidens.
> She considers a field and buys it;
> with the fruit of her hands she plants a vineyard.
> She clothes her loins with strength
> and makes her arms strong.

We identified the priorities for our lives and how we can manage our time according to those priorities.

We shared many practical suggestions on how to meet the needs of our families in terms of food, clothing, and an orderly home. We examined how to manage our home so that it is a place of peace, order, and beauty; how to cultivate our property as good stewards; and how to accomplish these tasks depending on the Lord's strength rather than struggling on our own. We also reviewed ways our ordinary experiences in homemaking enrich our experience of grace when we reflect on the sacraments.

This is the third set of six studies in the *Life-Nurturing Love* series: *Beloved and Blessed: Biblical Wisdom for Family Life*. We cover the topic of intimacy and how marital intimacy reflects the communion of the inner life of God. We share ways we can nurture affection for our spouse, which helps us to understand and embrace responsible parenthood. We consider how we can face the future with faith instead of fear, especially in the area of finances.

We reflect on ways God parents us and how we can imitate him as we parent our children. We share ways we can make a home for the Word as we teach our children the faith. And finally, we look at ways we can create a civilization of love in our home by loving and disciplining our children.

We are grateful you have chosen to be a part of the *Life-Nurturing Love* series. May the Lord bless you as you learn the faith more deeply and apply it in your marriage and family life.

PART ONE

The Heart

of Her Husband

Trusts in Her

1

Invitation to Intimacy

Chastity does not limit intimacy; it makes it possible. My parents have witnessed this for more than fifty years. Their loving, affectionate, and chaste relationship *before* marriage prepared the way for intimacy *in* marriage.

My husband, Scott, and I echo their sentiments. Throughout our engagement we had to temper our natural desire for passion with our God-given desire to honor our future spouse. Since our wedding in 1979, we have experienced both the beauty of God's design for marital intimacy and the power of purity in marital sexuality. And as my father says, "The best is yet to come."

How can we as married couples understand and share this vision with others, so that all of our marriages are enriched? How can we help husbands and wives feel beloved and blessed by their spouses? We begin with God—and the interpersonal communion he shares.

INTERPERSONAL COMMUNION WITHIN GOD

God is the Author of life, the communion of Persons: Father, Son, and Holy Spirit. Each pours himself out, one to the other, in life-giving, self-donating love. From the depths of this communion, God called us—man and woman—into being, made in his image. "Then God said, 'Let us make man in our image, after our likeness....' So God created man in

3

his own image, in the image of God he created him; male and female he created them" (Genesis 1:26a, 27). *God*, who is love, *destined us to long to love and be loved.* He gave us the joy and responsibility of loving, interpersonal communion with himself and each other.

PERSONAL INVITATION TO INTIMACY WITH GOD

Divine love (in Greek, *agape*) is unconditional love. It is a passionate, personal choice God makes to love and to forgive.[1] "We love, because he first loved us" (1 John 4:19). He invites us to intimacy with him.

From the beginning man and woman were "called to live in a communion of love, and in this way to mirror in the world the communion of love that is in God, through which the Three Persons love each other in the intimate mystery of the one divine life."[2] In our marriage God desires us to image him as a communion of life-giving Persons.

Original solitude and unity. Adam longed for Eve. When God paraded animals in front of Adam, he found no companion. Adam was perfect yet incomplete; he longed for communion with his own kind. He sought "a bond which is unique and definitive,"[3] an exclusive and indissoluble relationship.

When the Lord presented Eve to Adam, Adam exclaimed, "This at last is bone of my bones and flesh of my flesh; she shall be called Woman, because she was taken out of Man" (Genesis 2:23). Immediately the man recognized the gift that the woman was for him and vice versa. Overwhelmed with gratitude, man saw woman as the fulfillment of his desire to be united in love. This was not just a meeting of minds but a union of flesh. Together, *they* imaged God.

Marital blessings. God consecrated man and woman in marriage with a blessing that was also a command: "And God blessed them, and God said to them, 'Be fruitful and multiply, and fill the earth and subdue it; and have dominion over the fish of the sea and over the birds of the air and over every living thing that moves upon the earth'" (Genesis 1:28). This was not an ideal for a perfect world but the perennial teaching for marriage. After the flood God restated the same blessing-command to Noah, his wife, and their three sons and their wives (see Genesis 9:1).

In the Catholic Church the wedding vow includes the couple's commitment not only to a lifelong union but also to new life that emerges from that union.

This vision for marriage is radically different from that promoted by our secular society, whose focus is the moment and the couple. "This *mutual gift of the person in marriage* opens to the gift of a new life, *a new human being....* The spouses share in the creative power of God!"[4] Marital communion becomes a community of persons in our family.

INVITATION TO SPOUSAL INTIMACY

God enables our bodies to speak his life-giving language of love. Sex is God's idea; it is not the consequence of sin. In marital sexuality the *meaning* of unity is evident through *bonding,* the *purpose* of unity is evident in *babies,* and the *joy* of unity is evident through *pleasure.* Here is a brief look at each of these three aspects.

Unity through bonding. Marriage is the intimate unveiling of one another. "And the man and his wife were both naked, and were not ashamed" (Genesis 2:25). Husband and wife give and receive this gift of vulnerability through nakedness, approaching one another with awe and reverence. Their intimate act of marriage strengthens their bond. This bonding occurs independent of intent; even a prostitute, having sex only for pay, bonds with her partner (see 1 Corinthians 6:16). A couple bonds whether they think of sex as an isolated act, a part of a date, or an expression of lifelong commitment. This *is* reality.

Hollywood rarely depicts this reality. Talk show hosts guide guests with questions like, "Do you have sex on the first date? How long do you wait before you begin to cohabit? Do you even *want* to have children?" It is about the moment, rather than life together.

Jay Leno, in a "Jaywalking" bit, asked women about casual sex. "Do you ever go to bars to pick someone up?"

One woman said, "Every weekend."

Startled, he asked, "Do you even know their names?"

She immediately responded, "That would be *too* personal!"

Too personal to know their names, not too personal to have sex? My eyes welled up with tears—this young woman was someone's little girl. She had so much experience with sex and no clue what it was about.

Sex should not be the experience you live for with new partners or positions or pornography. Premarital sex creates an appetite for illicit sex that leaves spouses unprepared for routine in marital sexuality. Some people think that sex is fun *before* you marry, and then kiss it good-bye. A man was overheard at a wedding saying cynically, "There goes their sex life!"

Sex should not be reduced to mere biology, as if we were no different than animals being satisfied, whether or not we marry. A marriage license does not entitle one spouse to expect gratification of sexual desires regardless of the other's feelings. A misinformed college student stated, "I want to get married so I can have all the sex I want!"

We want to reclaim the truth about marital sexuality. We have the privilege of expressing profound truth with our bodies: *I am yours, and you are mine.* In marriage this bond is a blessing. We fulfill our longing to become one flesh, to give ourselves with abandon, and to receive the gift of the other.

Each intimate act of marriage renews our covenant. We become one flesh, which further unifies, strengthens, and fulfills our bond of love. Even our lovemaking can be a prayer. The wife's womb, like a sacred vessel, is set apart for consecrated use. The man is the high priest who enters the inner sanctuary, the holy of holies, within his wife.

He enables her womb to become a living tabernacle when he gives her his seed.

Love incarnated in babies. Giving your sexuality in service to God does not refer only to priests and nuns. As married persons, we also yield our sexuality to serve God. He gives us the grace we need to live the life to which he calls us. This includes our privilege in sharing in God's creative power. The two become one (see Genesis 2:24; Ephesians 5:31); and that one is so real, as my husband says, that nine months later you might have to give it a name! The child helps us visualize and deepen our union. We see our love incarnate in our cherished child.

Faithful, committed lifelong love creates the bond and mutual long-term support necessary for raising children. It provides the security of a stable marriage, capable of weathering the changes and challenges we face throughout life.

We receive each other in fruitful love, spiritual as well as physical. "[H]usband and wife, through that mutual gift of themselves, which is specific and exclusive to them alone, develop that union of two persons in which they perfect one another, cooperating with God in the generation and rearing of new lives."[5]

We share a profound and abiding love so that our conjugal fidelity will flourish. This love creates a "deep attachment of the heart which is expressed in action."[6] Thus the sanctity of marriage enables our family to become a "sanctuary of life."[7]

Each marriage is a new family. Even when no children result, "[the] marriage can radiate a fruitfulness of charity, of hospitality, and of sacrifice" (*CCC*, 1654).

The joy of unity—sensual and spiritual. When Adam first saw Eve, he recognized what husbands and wives should acknowledge: They are a gift to each other. "In God's eternal plan, woman is the one in whom the order of love in the created world of persons takes first root…. The Bridegroom is the one who loves. The Bride is loved: *it is she who receives love, in order to love in return.*"[8] This is a fully human love—an enduring and growing love to meet the demands of the vow.

Committed, marital love involves *sensuality*, through which we express physical attraction and desire, *sentimentality*, through which we enrich our emotional attachment, and *spirituality*, through which we help each other grow in virtue and faith.

Eros, the Greek word from which we derive *erotic*, is much richer in meaning than self-seeking pleasure. According to Pope Benedict XVI, "Evidently, *eros* needs to be disciplined and purified if it is to provide not just fleeting pleasure, but a certain foretaste of the pinnacle of our existence, of that beatitude for which our whole being yearns."[9] Purification and renunciation restore *eros* to "its true grandeur"[10] as we seek the good of our spouse.

IMITATION OF CHRIST

Remember Jesus' words, "He who finds his life will lose it, and he who loses his life for my sake will find it" (Matthew 10:39). We find ourselves by giving our lives for others, which requires great sacrifice. The radical message of the gospel applied to the act of marriage means we give ourselves in service and loving tenderness to the other, and the result is peace and joy.

Jesus' love for his bride reveals that love leads to life and life leads to sacrifice. "This human communion is confirmed, purified, and completed by communion in Jesus Christ, given through the sacrament of Matrimony. It is deepened by lives of the common faith and by the Eucharist received together" (*CCC*, 1644). This is part of our witness to the world—sacrificial, life-giving love!

SPOUSAL INVITATION TO INTIMACY

Joy in the physical act of marriage is pleasure *and* intimacy. If we pursue sex only for pleasure, it is empty and hollow. However, if we pursue the other's fulfillment, our pleasure is intense and deeply satisfying.

Marital sexuality has to fit into the overall context of marital life. Intimacy is only part—but a vital part—of our relationship. How can we be more available to each other? And how do we prepare for intimacy? Let's get specific.

Date time. Have you noticed that when caring for little ones demands the most time and energy, you have limited budgets for paying sitters and having dates? Rather than forgoing date time, see how creative you can be, given time and money constraints.

Perhaps you can pay a sitter and go on a free date, like attending a concert in the park, packing a picnic lunch or dinner to share in a secluded spot, or visiting a museum on a free day. Or you might enjoy participating once a week in a couples' sports team—like volleyball, soccer, or softball.

If you are blessed to live near grandparents, siblings, or other relatives who offer free baby-sitting, take their offer. Or maybe you could swap sitting with another couple every other weekend, so each couple could count on free sitting twice a month. It is important to keep dating your beloved.

Couch time. Choose a specific time you and your spouse can sit together, near your children, without their interrupting. (Obviously, this only works with children who understand the concept of not interrupting!) This might be brief—about fifteen minutes—right after work or dinner, to share about the day. Just be sure the conversation is not exclusively about the children.

You might opt for time after the children are in bed; however, if they do not see you enjoying each other, they might not know you are spending this time together. Seeing you desire time together—and getting it—helps children feel secure in their parents' love for each other.

Snitchin' in the kitchen. Snitchin' in the kitchen occurs when Dad sneaks up behind Mom to give her a hug or a smooch. This is not passion that makes children uncomfortable; this is being affectionate around them. Do not be fooled by feigned embarrassment by your kids! They love knowing Mom and Dad love each other. Let your children see your affection, your tenderness.

Scott and I were hugging in the kitchen when our son David, then age four, stepped between us. He was not separating us; he wanted to be included. "Let's squeeze!" he said. He wanted to feel the crush of love in the midst of our hug.

Fore-work. You need to prepare for intimacy as you prepare for Eucharistic Communion—physically, mentally, and spiritually. You might have heard of foreplay and even fore-talk. How about fore-work? If you are married I am sure you will recognize it.

One of the most romantic things a man can do is clean out the garage, go to the store for a few items, or do the dishes. These small acts of service express marital love, of which intimacy is a part.

If your spouse loves order, and your bedroom (the last dumping ground) is a mess, perhaps you could do a quick pickup. Then lower the visibility of any remaining disorder with candlelight. A nice spray for sheets, available at bath-and-body stores, can add to the ambiance. Or perhaps set the mood with good music and a glass of wine to demonstrate your desire to please your beloved.

Instead of jumping into bed wearing sweatpants and a T-shirt, consider changing to a feminine nightgown. Unlike something a prostitute might wear, lingerie includes nightgowns that highlight your features in an attractive way and sets the tone for intimacy.

One gentleman, married for more than fifty years, said that after groceries the most important purchase should be women's lingerie. "When my wife rounds the corner from our bathroom to our bedroom in lingerie, I've just got to know what's underneath!"

At my wedding showers I received several nightgowns. Mom suggested that I put some away for the next year, since our budget would not include lingerie for a while.

Later I enjoyed wearing something new without spending money.

Fore-talk. Sometimes you cannot make love until you have talked about your day. This can be the difference between "having sex," where you feel used, and "making love." Your interaction with your spouse that day may affect your openness to each other. If you had conflict between you, stress from finances, a tough day at work, or criticism from someone, you need resolution before you can physically express love.

Men and women are not physiologically wired the same way. It is important to talk about what you like and do not like in making love. Think through the five senses; list your turn-ons and turnoffs. Then respectfully share your lists with each other. You might be surprised at what pleases or bothers the other.

Use the language of intimacy—not foul talk—to tell your husband how much you desire him or to tell your wife how much she pleases you. Read through the Bible's Song of Solomon for lavish descriptions of romantic love, the celebration of sexual desire, and the anticipation of enjoyment between husband and wife. This is sacred Scripture, yet it reveals the yearning of marital lovers.

Fore-play. Marital sexuality is an art, not a science. It takes a lifetime to learn to express love physically, especially given a woman's many physiological changes. If a husband gains the knowledge of how to touch his wife so that they both experience pleasure, he will find greater pleasure. His patience will enable her to respond in a way that he longs for her to respond. Working together to express their love for the sake of the other prevents either spouse from feeling used or neglected.

"The Lovemaking Cycle," from Christopher and Rachel McCluskey's book *When Two Become One,*[11] describes marital intimacy in a four-stage process: *Atmosphere, Arousal, Apex,* and *Afterglow.*

Atmosphere sets the stage for expressing intimacy. The time and energy you offer along with privacy enhance that atmosphere. A lock on your door may help you relax, knowing a child cannot surprise you. (That is both for your good and for your child's well-being.)

Arousal refers to a certain playfulness you enjoy together. Pay attention to the senses. Do you need to wash before being together? Would it help to brush your teeth or request that of your spouse? Men, might it help to shave a second time so that she can enjoy your smooth face? Women, might it help to shave either for his pleasure or for your own sense of being more attractive? The better you feel about your appearance and the thoughtfulness of your spouse, the more you communicate your desire and preparation to be together. This allows for passion to build.

Apex is the height of physical and emotional release. The act of marriage increases your physical and spiritual connection as you surrender control of your responses to the delight of your spouse.

Afterglow is time holding each other close, resting in each other's arms. Bask in the warmth of tender affection and life-giving love. This is a time to affirm your spouse, thankful for tenderness and vulnerability.

If you do not have much time, or if one of you feels sick, tired, or too busy, you may want to postpone your plans or make it quick. But just as you cannot build a strong body with a steady diet of junk food, so you will not strengthen your marriage with "quickies" as a steady course of lovemaking.

Your goal is sweet, intimate communion for faithful and fruitful, lifelong love.

CHAPTER TWO

Challenges to Intimacy

A merican culture depicts sex as more exciting than ever with newly enhanced genitalia, new positions, new drugs, and even new partners to increase pleasure. In contrast, marital sexuality is caricatured as boring, dull, and routine. What is the truth?

The truth is that when married couples *do* face challenges in lovemaking, it is not about having better sex—as though it were a thing to acquire. It is about loving your spouse better and reveling in intimacy. A married couple does not live for sex. Although very significant, sex is only one aspect of their life together.

Though problems with marital intimacy can exist, rarely are they addressed. Whether they be spiritual, physical, interpersonal, or psychological, there is no area—including loving each other physically—that we cannot bring to God in prayer. He cares about every facet of our lives, which is *why* we want to examine obstacles in expressing marital intimacy. We want God to strengthen all Christian couples with a blessed marriage in every way, including sexual intimacy.

SPIRITUAL CHALLENGES

Spiritual challenge #1: Is pleasure allowed? Man did not invent sex; God did. From the beginning God gave man and woman the gift of marital sexuality. That is why sexual love that expresses the intimate and chaste union of husband and wife, open to life, is "noble and worthy."[1]

Our sex-obsessed culture elevates sex as the ultimate high while denigrating it as a life-affirming or life-creating event. Some treat sex as if it were good exercise; one teen said, "It's like playing basketball!" A college coed equated it with "getting to know a person to see *if* you want to risk dating!" Countless TV shows and movies demonstrate how meaningless sex can be, as nearly anonymous couples toss across the sheets. The point is, they have *no* clue what meaningful sex is.

Our sex-saturated culture cannot understand *why* couples would want to make love after thirty years. *Intimacy* is what they do not understand; sexuality is so much richer and more fulfilling than what this world presents.

The Old Testament refers to marital sexuality as *knowing* someone: "Now Adam knew Eve his wife, and she conceived and bore Cain" (Genesis 4:1a). My dad says this is why, after fifty years of marriage, the sex life between him and my mom keeps getting better. "I *know* her better, and I *love* her more!"

My father, a minister, was counseling a woman, and she converted to Christianity. Since her husband was not a believer, she became uncomfortable having sex. Dad reminded her that she should not neglect this vital part of her marriage as a Christian wife, regardless of her husband's faith.

A few weeks later the husband made an appointment to see Dad. Once there, the husband said, "I just want to know what you told my wife! Our sex life has never been better. I want whatever she has."

"I told her not to be so spiritual that she would neglect the physical relationship with you," my father said. "Jesus is the reason your wife is loving you. And I'd love to introduce you to Jesus." And he did.

Spiritual challenge #2: cure for concupiscence. Concupiscence refers to our inclination to sin, or as the Council of Trent put it, "the tinder for sin" (*CCC*, no. 1264, Council of Trent, DS 1515). Saint Paul refers to the act of marriage as a cure for the concupiscence in sexual desire: "To the unmarried and the widows I say that it is well for them to remain single as I do. But if they cannot exercise self-control, they should marry. For it is better to marry than to be aflame with passion" (1 Corinthians 7:8–9). In other words, if you have passionate love for someone, get married. It is not sinful to desire a faithful and fruitful union with your spouse.

At the same time, Pope John Paul II warned against committing the sin of lust, even with your spouse. It is possible to misuse each other, even when you are open to life. "A love which is not 'fairest,' but reduced only to the satisfaction of concupiscence (cf. 1 Jn 2:16), or to a man's and a woman's mutual 'use' of each other, makes persons *slaves to their weaknesses.*"[2]

Some perceive marital sexuality as an indignity to endure only for the greater good of conceiving a child. Then they withhold themselves from their spouse during pregnancy or stop relations all together once menopause occurs, since they cannot see a point to relations. To view the act of marriage as merely a cure for concupiscence or a way to create babies reduces a spouse simply to a means to an end, which is against love.

Spiritual challenge #3: power play with conjugal duty. We have a conjugal duty to give our bodies to each other in the act of marriage; however, if we *demand* sex regardless of our spouse's feelings or wishes, we *contradict* what is intended as an act of love.

The husband should give to his wife her conjugal rights, and likewise the wife to her husband. For the wife does not rule over her own body, but the husband does; likewise the husband does not rule over his own body, but the wife does. Do not refuse one another except perhaps by agreement for a season, that you may devote yourselves to prayer; but then come together again, lest Satan tempt you through lack of self-control. (1 Corinthians 7:3–5)

Spouses sin against each other when they misuse this gift of marital sexuality, either by refusing or demanding to make love. This is a shift from *desiring to give ourselves freely* to *demanding our rights.*

Saint Paul includes a stern warning: Do not let Satan get a foothold! A spouse can never excuse adultery on the basis of neglect. But withholding ourselves from our spouse can create vulnerability for temptation. The question is, how can we be more available to our spouse? If our model is the relationship between Christ and the Church, what does either withhold from the other? Nothing!

Spiritual challenge #4: lack of tenderness later in life. "Jane Doe" requested I share her plight as an empty-nester: "Our sexual life ceased, and we no longer touched or hugged. Our evenings became a series of TV programs, the news, and computer interest. Our intimate conversations ceased, and we didn't even dream dreams together. Older years should not be like this. This is very sad."

I'm sure this could be written by a man too. I see many lonely men who wish their wives would be more attentive.

This woman's husband has communicated a type of abandonment. As we age, will we nurture our love or neglect it? Will we grow old together, or will we grow apart? Even when sexual intercourse is no longer life-giving, it continues to be life-nurturing as we express tender interpersonal communion.

PHYSICAL CHALLENGES

What physical obstacles do couples face in marital intimacy? Is help available?

Physical challenge #1: medical issues. A wife's medical concerns can include hormonal imbalances from her menstrual cycle, ovulation pain, pregnancy nausea, or other difficulties. She might have discomfort or pain after delivery or miscarriage. These challenges should be addressed by an OB/GYN or a Natural Family Planning consultant. The Pope Paul VI Institute has helped numerous women with gynecological health issues.[3]

A husband's medical concerns might include difficulty completing the act of marriage due to erectile dysfunction and performance anxiety, or inability to physically satisfy his wife because of premature ejaculation. These problems may require more time for sexual intercourse or medical assistance.

Physical challenge #2: pain during intercourse. Some women experience pain during their first acts of intercourse, after a miscarriage or delivery, or during menopause. If the pain is caused by dryness, K-Y Jelly can be helpful following foreplay, but excessive dryness may require a prescription for vaginal estrogen. Pain from tension may be eased with a glass of wine and taking more time for foreplay. Placing a pillow under the small of a woman's back can alleviate discomfort or pressure and provide a better angle. Communicate your concerns to each other, and contact a specialist as needed.

Physical challenge #3: fatigue. When a mother has been up all night with a baby and unable to nap, she may be too tired to make love. A wise husband could seize this opportunity for "fore-work" by tending the baby after dinner while his wife refreshes herself with a nap.

Physical challenge #4: changing body shape. Bodies change during pregnancy. Some women return to their normal stomach size quickly but continue to adjust to enlarged breasts. Others struggle for months or years to lose extra pounds and inches. It takes time to become comfortable with a new shape.

A husband may need to alter his expectations about his wife's postpartum looks. He should be compassionate, realizing the sacrifices she has made to bear life.

Wives want to look good after having a baby, but why should our goal be to look as if we never had a baby *when we did?* Accommodations need to be made. In Europe curvaceous women are appreciated. Our goal should be to look like women, not prepubescent teens.

With my first baby the doctor noticed that I was unhappy about my stretch marks. He told me that some African tribes *honor* a woman with stretch marks for the sacrifices she made to bear a child.

A friend and I delivered babies on the same day. After our six-week postdelivery exams, I asked her, "Did you get the all-clear?"

She responded tentatively. "Yes,...but when I told my husband, he just said, 'I can't get into it until you lose those last five pounds off your hips!'"

I wanted to slug him! How dare he withhold himself from his loving wife until she looked a certain way?

In stark contrast, my husband has said numerous times, "Your body says you have loved me enough to bear my children!" God bless Scott for those encouraging words. I hope other men echo them to their wives.

INTERPERSONAL CHALLENGES

Interpersonal challenge #1: communicating desire. When it comes to how different we are as men and women, we usually think, "Vive la difference!" However, some differences complicate communication. Perhaps he gives overt sexual advances; she wants more romantic, playful, or relational cues. Some like to schedule time for intimacy; others prefer spontaneity. (TV and movies aside, spontaneity is not the norm. Many women need time to prepare before expressing love.)

Regardless of differences in perspective, work through them by sharing your thoughts. Communication is essential to a satisfying sex life.

Interpersonal challenge #2: different internal clocks. What if one of you is a morning person and one is a night person? In dating, couples accommodate various schedules so that they can be together. However, once married, each may respond to his or her own internal clock.

That makes a difference in marital intimacy. A night owl may not want to be woken at dawn by an early bird; intimacy is not on the agenda—more sleep is. The night owl may be irritated to find his early bird already asleep. He is ready for her, but she is out. One couple met in the middle: When their kids were in school, he would take his lunch break at home so that they could make love.

Timing becomes even trickier when dealing with pregnancy tiredness or little ones who climb into bed. Talk about timing.

Interpersonal challenge #3: different needs. What happens when physical touch and closeness is *not* your love language (see chapter ten for information on love languages) *but it is his—and* you have been touched all day by children? You may be inclined to make love less, unless you think through differences in your and your spouse's needs.

My mom, cautiously but directly, asked about my frequency of lovemaking—not for an amount, but was I regularly meeting my husband's physical needs? Her questions were very helpful. (Few people could do that.)

Perhaps you can allow me to ask you: Are you meeting your husband's physical needs? Is it possible that you are on sensory overload from the children? Do you listen for his needs, which he may whisper while the children shout? Do you catch his cues for physical touch and closeness?

Marital intimacy helps us reaffirm our unconditional love for our spouse. Each of us feels safe in the arms of our beloved. This can be healing during a time of grief, when we have feelings of inadequacy, or when we suffer from others' criticisms.

In St. Louis I asked a crowd to consider the following: If frequent reception of the Eucharist strengthens your relationship with the Lord, what might frequent reception of your spouse do? A woman cornered me afterward. "I know what you're saying! But I told my husband that once a month is good enough for me, and it better be good enough for him!"

I simply asked, "What did *he* say?" She stalked away.

Frequency is not something we announce but a decision we make jointly. Men and women vary in expectations. Currently our culture treats a man's desire for intercourse as almost animalistic, but it is a God-given drive. It is stronger in those men whose primary love language is physical touch (and it is for many men).

Pope John Paul II addressed the problem of not caring about the other's gratification:

> If a woman does not obtain natural gratification from the sexual act there is a danger that her experience of it will be qualitatively inferior, will not involve her fully as a person. This sort of experience makes nervous reactions only too likely, and may for instance cause secondary sexual frigidity. Frigidity is sometimes the result of an inhibition on the part of the woman herself, or of a lack of involvement which may even at times be her own fault. But it is usually the result of egoism in the man, who failing to recognize the subjective desires of the woman in intercourse, and the objective laws of the sexual process taking place in her, seeks merely his own satisfaction, sometimes quite brutally.[4]

There is nothing wrong when a wife desires to be satisfied by her husband.

Interpersonal challenge #4: different sexual cycles. A man's sexual cycle can be as brief as response and release in minutes. A woman's can include phases of a monthly cycle, pregnancy, delivery and nursing, and menopause. These differences highlight the complexities of marital intimacy as opposed to one-night stands.

Should you abstain from intercourse when the woman has her period? Leviticus 15 clarified that intercourse during menstruation ceremonially defiled both the man and woman. Instead they were to abstain for seven days and then abstain for seven more days from the time her flow stopped. Interesting note: If a couple abstained during her menstrual flow plus seven days, when were they making love? Most likely when the woman was ovulating, and the man's sperm supply would be ample after such a time of abstinence.

This law does not apply today. Still, many women feel unclean, uncomfortable, bloated, and unattractive during their periods. This may be a good time to abstain. Let your spouse know how you feel.

Interpersonal challenge #5: lack of privacy. When the marriage bed becomes the family bed with the arrival of the first baby, many men feel displaced. They know they have to adjust to less time and attention from their wives, but if the baby is always in their bed, *where* is the place for intimacy?

When one husband was struggling with his wife's nursing in bed, someone suggested he take the bedroom down the hall—definitely *not* a thoughtful response. Another encouraged the wife to hear her husband's heart and care about both his needs and the baby's, without neglecting either—a much wiser approach.

Since marriage is the primary relationship in the family, we need to make sexual intimacy in marriage a priority. We want healthy boundaries in terms of privacy and time. Little ones can handle some separation from their parents, and a couple should never make love with a little one in their bed. So put your baby in the crib for a while, and enjoy time together.

PSYCHOLOGICAL CHALLENGES

Psychological challenge #1: past trauma. You may have experienced trauma from illicit relationships in which you chose to participate. Or you may have experienced sexual abuse or even rape. Perhaps you have been traumatized by sexual indiscretions of your parents or by ways in which their broken relationship left you insecure.

Such pain and scars rarely disappear simply by saying one more novena. In these situations you may need counseling for healing. The greater the wholeness you bring to your marriage and parenting, the better for everyone in your family.

Psychological challenge #2: false guilt. Before a couple weds, shame plays a key role in keeping relationships healthy, safeguarding the dignity of the other person. In fact, shame "is a matter *not* just of protecting but of *revealing* the value of the person."[5] Consequently premarital sex has two damaging aspects: physical shamelessness, which is a rejection of what is best for the other person for sexual gratification; and emotional shamelessness, which is a refusal to protect the feelings and the body of the other person.

Sometimes spouses continue to have feelings of shame, but that is not appropriate. True love swallows up shame. Like Adam and Eve in their original unity, married couples are free to revel in nakedness unashamed.

Some people feel uncomfortable with the out-of-control feelings in lovemaking. This is a kind of false modesty.

Spouses should guard their hearts from lust, even with their spouse. However, they should not equate a genuine passion for their beloved with lust. Instead they can pray for abandonment to joy with their beloved.

Psychological challenge #3: fears. You may have fears of pregnancy, miscarriage, delivery, feeling overwhelmed, or recurring postpartum depression. These fears are real. They need to be addressed by medical personnel as well as others who have been in your situation.

Fear can be lessened through information. Perhaps you want to switch from a doctor to a midwife or from a midwife to a doctor next time you have a baby. Maybe you could change the location of your next delivery to a birthing center, a hospital, or your home. You have choices of anesthesia for delivery and whether or not you want to be induced. If you have had C-sections in the past, you can research the VBAC (Vaginal Birth After Cesarean) option or plan your next C-section. Perhaps you can find medications or advice to help with postpartum depression.

A friend suffered from postpartum depression for almost six weeks, offering up the angst of desiring her child yet not wanting to be with her. Finally she shared her agony and found help through the Pope Paul VI Institute. The staff worked with local hospital personnel, and through blood tests they diagnosed the underlying problem and came up with a remedy. Within hours (not days) prescribed medication relieved severe symptoms, and within days the depression was almost eliminated.

We *can* face fears if we train our hearts in truth. Why do we want to be open to life? What is the value of each life?

To bear a child for the Lord is a great privilege. Following each of my deliveries, I reviewed these important thoughts to quell my concerns and to focus on the gift of each child. This is not mind-over-matter self-talk. I was elevating my thoughts above my pain to the joy and privilege of bearing new life.

It was one thing to *state* my desire to continue being open to life. It was another to pull myself out of a hospital bed after my latest C-section, walk across the floor (hoping the staples kept everything together), and *still* maintain that desire. As every step shot internal pain to places unknown, I would wonder if I could make it back to bed without sobbing. I was not thinking about the next child, just basic survival, grateful for every push of morphine the nurses allowed. Yet God's grace sustained me, moment by moment, helping me to make the pain and discomfort a prayer.

After I brought Jeremiah home from the hospital, I thought I was doing pretty well training my heart in truth. Then Hannah took a peek at the baby in my arms, her third brother, and said matter-of-factly, "Maybe the next one will be a girl."

I cringed! There was only one way there could be another —if I was willing to go through all of this again. My face contorted; I looked away quickly as I said, "Yes, honey, maybe the next one will be a girl." I thought, *Lord, I need you to work in my heart so there can be another one.* Then I committed to reviewing all that was good, true, and lovely about openness to life, so that my heart would be ready to receive the gift of another child.

Five weeks later I caught myself thinking wistfully about the maternity clothes I was packing away, wondering when or even if I would ever *get* to wear them again. I realized, by God's grace, that my heart echoed my words. Another baby really would be an amazing blessing, worth all of the pain and effort to bring her (or him) into the world.

Psychological Challenge #4: stress. Stress can interfere with sexual relations. Maybe you face financial problems, from loss of a job, not setting a budget, or not following one you have. You may experience tensions at work or be frustrated by caring for children without a break, especially if either of you fails to appreciate different ways the other serves the family.

You may have stress from trying to get pregnant or trying not to. You may feel stress over a child's issues, especially a child in pain or one who acts badly, creating a wedge between you and your spouse. A spirit of accusation between you, related to a child's injury or behavior, adds difficulties that are self-destructive psychologically and emotionally.

During times of great stress, you and your spouse can feel pulled apart. You need wisdom and practical solutions. Communicate your concerns, and pray together. You may also benefit from counseling.

All of these challenges can make it difficult to imagine making love. However, the act of marriage *objectively* expresses the unity you have in the sacrament of marriage, whether or not you feel it. Though you may feel like pulling away from your spouse, it may be more helpful to increase your frequency of intercourse. You do not want to substitute making love for resolving problems, but neither do you want additional problems by not making love enough. Commit to loving each other physically because of your need to be united.

The best gift we can give our children is true, lasting, tender love for our spouse. When children know that their Mom and Dad really love each other, they feel secure.

SINS AGAINST MARITAL CHASTITY

Inappropriate sexual acts. Some couples act as if any sexual acts are licit as long as they are married. This is not so. Saint Paul warns, "Let marriage be held in honor among all, and let the marriage bed be undefiled; for God will judge the immoral and adulterous" (Hebrews 13:4). There *are* inappropriate sexual acts that defile the marriage bed.

Your marriage bed is the most sacred place in your home. Without getting specific, let me be clear: Sperm only goes where it can be life-giving in the wife. *Nothing* else is licit! Anything else is objectively evil, according to the *Catechism of the Catholic Church* (see *CCC*, 2351). Present this to your spouse and talk it through.

Contraception or sterilization. Every act of marriage is to be open to life. Contraception and sterilization—in order not to conceive—are serious sins. But it is not a sin if for medical reasons you take the pill or have a hysterectomy.

Abortion. If you or your spouse has been involved in an abortion, this can affect intimacy in ways you do not understand. I want you to know that healing is possible. The Lord wants to restore you in wholeness as well as holiness. I highly recommend Rachel's Vineyard, an outstanding ministry that is helping hundreds of couples find hope and healing in the context of a weekend retreat.[6]

Pornography. At a conference in Anaheim, a woman questioned me, "My husband has asked me to view some X-rated films so we can learn how to make love better. Is that right?"

"Absolutely not," I replied. "Pornography does not teach you about love but about lust. It does not teach you how to honor your spouse but how to use your spouse like an object. Burn them—don't throw them away, or someone may find them. And tell your husband, 'Never again!'"

Pornography is quasi-adultery: You are aroused by someone to whom you are not married, then you use your spouse to satisfy your lust. Pornography poisons intimacy.

You and your spouse do not need pornography to learn techniques of lovemaking. Inexperience means you are novices in the art of physical love and affection. And the good news is that this is learn-by-doing, on-the-job training. You have a lifetime to learn together how to love each other.

Intimacy flows from and strengthens your entire marital relationship. If pornography is a part of either your or your spouse's life, please contact the National Coalition for the Protection of Children & Families or Sexaholics Anonymous.[7] Please get help to break this dangerous addiction before it destroys you and those whom you love.

Be aware that even without pornography, selfishness and the misuse of your spouse are still possible. It is vital to learn self-control for those times when it is inadvisable to make love: during an illness, a threat of miscarriage, post-partum recovery, or recovery from an injury.

Adultery. When people are unfaithful in marriage, they damage their relationship to God as well as harm their entire family (see Malachi 2:13–16). Adultery shatters the foundation of trust on which marriage is built. It is very difficult for the other spouse to risk vulnerability again, but it *is* possible. "The Holy Spirit is the seal of their covenant, the ever-available source of their love and the strength to renew their fidelity" (*CCC*, 1624). Draw on the Spirit's strength and grace to enable forgiveness to flow and accountability to begin the rebuilding process.

A particular movement that is helping couples rebuild trust in their marriages is called Retrouvaille.[8] This ministry is for couples in marital crisis. Through Retrouvaille many marriages and families have been spared the agony of divorce and have seen meaningful family life restored.

FAN THE FLAMES OF PASSION!

Wives, set your hearts on your beloved, and you will be blessed. Be thankful for the joy of loving and being loved in a faithful and fruitful union.

Husbands, desire your beloved always, and you will be blessed. "Rejoice in the wife of your youth.... Let her affection fill you at all times with delight, be infatuated always with her love" (Proverbs 5:18b, 19b).

Ask the Lord to help you express your love physically in a way that pleases him and honors your spouse. He wants to enable you to nurture the fountain of love and life in your family.

PART TWO

Her Children

Rise Up and

Call Her Blessed

CHAPTER THREE

Family as the Sanctuary of Life

God designed marital sexuality to bond husband and wife to one another *and*, with their cooperation, to create a new human being—a baby. God enables their bodies to speak his language of love so they become life-giving lovers and life-loving givers. This communion of persons becomes a community of persons. Therefore, *every act of marriage is to be open to life.*

CHILDREN ARE GIFTS

Children are *only* and *always* blessings.

> Behold, sons are a heritage from the LORD,
>   the fruit of the womb a reward.
> Like arrows in the hand of a warrior
>   are the sons of one's youth.
> Happy is the man who has
>   his quiver full of them! (Psalm 127:3–5a)

According to Pope Benedict XVI, "The Lord gives the gift of children, seen as a blessing and grace, a sign *of life* that continues and *of the history of salvation* moving toward new stages…. Procreation is, therefore, a gift bearing life and well-being for society."[1]

The psalmist describes a blessed man:

Your wife will be like a fruitful vine
　　within your house;
your children will be like olive shoots
　　around your table.
Behold, thus shall the man be blessed
　　who fears the LORD. (Psalm 128:3–4)

The Proverbs 31 woman exemplifies this: Her children have the maturity to "rise up and call her blessed" (Proverbs 31:28).

Each child refracts the beauty of our love in a different way. When my friend's husband was tragically killed, she faced widowhood with eight children ranging from fourteen years to fourteen months. She was so grateful for all of them. "Each child reflects something different about my beloved."

A child is not a possession to acquire or an adventure to take; he or she is a gift to receive. "A child does not come from outside as something added on to the mutual love of the spouses, but springs from the very heart of mutual giving, as its fruit and fulfillment" (*CCC*, 2366). A child enables us to fall in love all over again. The child is a gift of God flowing from the heart of marital love; this is just as true with adoption as with a child born from our union.

Children are not the penalty you pay for enjoying sex. Nor is God the consummate spoilsport saying, you can have sex, but you are going to have to have children! Rather God allows us to enjoy intimacy in the depths of our physical union. *And* he may even gift us with a child as a fruit of that love—a bonus.

Children are "the supreme gift of marriage and contribute

very substantially to the welfare of their parents."[2] We know *we* contribute to *their* well-being. We do not bring them from the hospital and announce, "Your bedroom's second on the left, food's in the fridge,…" We understand their dependence on us. But *they* contribute to *our* well-being, providing sacrificial opportunities for us to grow more like Christ (see 1 Timothy 2:15).

COMMUNION IN THE MYSTERY OF LIFE

Women are given a great privilege in pregnancy: a communion with the very mystery of life, a world within. "The moral and spiritual strength of a woman is joined to her awareness that *God entrusts the human being to her in a special way.*"[3]

We experience such joy as we ponder the development of our child (see Psalm 139). We can be in a crowd and suddenly feel the baby move; no one notices we are communing with our little one. For nine months we anticipate the revelation of this new person.

When a woman bears a child, she nurtures the life within her physically, emotionally, psychologically, and spiritually. "It is therefore necessary that *the man* be fully aware that in their shared parenthood he *owes a special debt to the woman.*"[4] She draws her husband into the mystery of life, since "in many ways he has to *learn* his own *'fatherhood' from the mother.*"[5] The husband, for his part, "should be responsibly committed to providing attention and support throughout the pregnancy and, if possible, at the moment of birth."[6]

The labor and delivery of our child is a "paschal sign,"[7] which mirrors Christ's self-offering and resurrection. We offer our lives so that our child may live now *and* live forever. Our child's genealogy includes not only our genealogies but also an eternal genealogy beginning in and returning to God.

To Everything a Purpose

God has given a purpose for each thing he has made. For our moral sexual health, we must act in accord with the purpose God intends for marital intimacy. With love and a well-formed conscience, we examine our actions in light of nature, reason, virtue, and the dignity of the human person.

John Kippley, in *Sex and the Marriage Covenant*, explains natural law with a helpful food analogy. Why do we eat? We eat because we are hungry, want flavor, feel celebratory, or even feel upset. But we would only eat something undesirable if it were nutritious, to sustain our lives.

In ancient Rome, feasts offered more than people could eat. If the people were full but wanted to eat more, they would use vomitoriums—tall vases in the corners of the room in which they could vomit—then indulge more.

Today we refer to such misuse of food, either by overeating and throwing up (bulimia) or by starving (anorexia), as eating *disorders*. We do so because they are *not ordered* to the primary purpose of food, which is nutrition. Likewise, if we indulge in marital sexuality while denying its fruitfulness, our actions are disordered.

Why do we have sexual relations? We experience physical unity, conceive new life, and enjoy the pleasure of sex. We can experience unity and pleasure in other ways in marriage, but the purpose unique to marital sexuality is conceiving new life.

In the marriage covenant we have the possibility of speaking the most profound truth we can speak with our bodies: I am a gift to you, and I receive you as a gift, completely and fully. That gift includes our fertility.

What are we really saying when, in the midst of marital intimacy, we stop to get our barriers in place? With contraception we are saying, "I love my husband, but I reject the life-giving nature of his seed." Or, "I love my wife, but I reject the life-nurturing nature of her womb." Whether or not intended, instead of speaking our bodies' most profound truth of total gift of self, we turn it into a lie! According to moral theologian Dr. Janet Smith, "Contraception is not a rational or natural act… [I]t severs having sex from having babies and allows millions to participate in an act whose consequences they are not prepared to face."[8]

Contraceptive marital intercourse is feasting on love and then vomiting the contents. Contraception is not just a bad choice. (Eating a cherry Popsicle without guarding your white shirt from drips is a bad choice.) Contraception severs our relationship with God. Like Adam and Eve, we are determining good and evil, declaring sterilized sex to be good and life-giving love to be avoided at all costs. Where is God in this decision?

THE WITNESS OF SCRIPTURE

Does Scripture address contraception? Due to modern technology, most people assume that contraception is only a recent issue. Certainly many advances have occurred in the last hundred years. However, ancient Egyptians made spermicidal vaginal suppositories, ancient Persians inserted sea sponges soaked in spermicidal fluids, and the ancient Arabs' practice of inserting small stones into their camels' uteri to prohibit pregnancy was imitated by others on humans with various small objects (similar to today's I.U.D.).[9] And Scripture describes *coitus interruptus*:

> And Judah took a wife for Er his first-born, and her name was Tamar. But Er, Judah's first-born, was wicked in the sight of the LORD; and the LORD slew him. Then Judah said to Onan, "Go in to your brother's wife, and perform the duty of a brother-in-law to her, and raise up offspring for your brother." But Onan knew that the offspring would not be his; so when he went in to his brother's wife he spilled the semen on the ground, lest he should give offspring to his brother. And what he did was displeasing in the sight of the LORD, and he slew him also. (Genesis 38:6–10)

God punished Onan's sin with death. What was his sin? Onan intentionally spilled his semen on the ground, that is, he contracepted. Last century's school books, in teaching about confession, referred to the sin of contraception as "Onanism."

THE UNCHANGED AND UNCHANGING WITNESS OF THE CHURCH

Until 1930 all Orthodox and Protestant churches concurred with the Catholic Church's consistent witness for two thousand years: Contraception is counter to God's plan. Then the Lambeth Conference of the Anglican Church in England voted to allow birth control for extreme cases. Contraception would be permitted only if the mother's life would be endangered by conceiving and the couple's ability to abstain for the rest of their marriage was impractical.

That same year Pope Pius XII promulgated a new document, *On Christian Marriage,* in which he stated unequivocally:

> Since, therefore, openly departing from the uninterrupted Christian tradition some recently have judged it possible solemnly to declare another doctrine regarding this question, the Catholic Church, to whom God has entrusted the defense of the integrity and purity of morals, standing erect in the midst of the moral ruin which surrounds her, in order that she may preserve the chastity of the nuptial union from being defiled by this foul stain, raises her voice in token of her divine ambassadorship and through Our mouth proclaims anew: any use whatsoever of matrimony exercised in such a way that the act is deliberately frustrated in its natural power to generate life is an offense against the law of God and of nature, and those who indulge in such are branded with the guilt of a grave sin.[10]

Whether or not someone clearly taught this to you, it is essential for you to understand: Both contraception and sterilization are intrinsically evil acts.

THE LORDSHIP OF JESUS CHRIST

Jesus wants us to yield everything to him: our heart, mind, soul, and body—*including our fertility.* Sometimes we respond with more of an independent American spirit than a heartfelt expression of faith. *I can manage my fertility, Lord; you can take care of the rest.* Saint Paul tells us that our bodies are temples that should not be desecrated: "Do you not know that your body is a temple of the Holy Spirit within you, which you have from God? You are not your own; you were bought with a price. So glorify God in your body" (1 Corinthians 6:19–20).

We want to honor God in our bodies through marital chastity. Still, how many Christians flounder either because we are not living this truth well or have not shared it?

> Trust in the LORD with all your heart,
>   and do not rely on your own insight.
> In all your ways acknowledge him,
>   and he will make straight your paths.
> Be not wise in your own eyes;
>   fear the LORD, and turn away from evil.
> It will be healing to your flesh
>   and refreshment to your bones. (Proverbs 3:5–8)

This is *Christian* truth, not just Catholic truth!

Living sacrifices. How do we live this beautiful design for marriage? We embrace our call to be living sacrifices. "I appeal to you therefore, brethren, by the mercies of God, to present your bodies as a living sacrifice, holy and acceptable to God, which is your spiritual worship" (Romans 12:1). God's mercy helps us *keep* the law, rather than exempting us from it.

He calls us to be living sacrifices *in our bodies,* not just our hearts or minds. Pregnancy brings this into sharp focus. We may choose to be open to life, but many involuntary sacrifices follow: nausea, stretch marks, varicose veins, and so on. And there are sacrifices for us to make in the delivery and care for each child.

Our sacrificial love is an expression of worship. This is the physical side of being spiritual. Why is it so difficult? We are not yet dead! When the sacrifice becomes difficult, we begin to crawl off the altar. Then God gently draws us back, promising his grace that we might continue to imitate his selfless love.

Transformed thinking. We are so saturated in our time and culture that we *cannot* avoid being influenced by it, unless we use thoughtful reflection. "Do not be conformed to this world but be transformed by the renewal of your mind, that you may prove what is the will of God, what is good and acceptable and perfect" (Romans 12:2). The key is transformed thinking.

Bank tellers are trained to recognize counterfeit money by touching a lot of genuine dollar bills. Likewise, we recognize error more readily by filling our minds with truth. Then we will understand God's will for our lives.

MIXED REACTIONS FROM CATHOLICS

The 1960s were a turbulent time for sexual morality. Many Catholics thought the Church would adopt modern ideas about birth control. On July 29, 1968, Pope Paul VI promulgated his encyclical *Humanae Vitae.* He addressed the Church's duty, as "guardian and interpreter" of the whole moral law, to teach the truth about marital sexuality. Then he clarified what the consistent, coherent teaching of the Church had been and would continue to be. He faithfully proclaimed these timeless truths to a new generation.

That same day a group of American priests and theologians participated in a well-orchestrated, worldwide dissent, emboldening opponents of Pope Paul VI. They wanted to silence faithful priests. Confusion ensued. Today many Catholics feel they have been misinformed; they are frustrated, confused, angry, or sad.

Misinformed. Even after eight to twelve years of Catholic schooling, some Catholics realize they were not taught the truth about sexual morality. Some received poor catechesis from those who either did not understand Church teaching or, worse, deliberately dissented from *Humanae Vitae.* Catholics were taught to "follow their conscience," which meant, if they felt contraception was OK, it was.

We should follow our consciences once we have formed them according to truth. Our practices should reflect our renewed understanding. We need to understand Church teaching to appreciate how our bodies fulfill God's will. Then we can counter false teaching by faithfully living and proclaiming the truth.

Frustrated. Unclear messages, even in the confessional, are frustrating. One priest said, "God love you— you're doing the best you can. You have several children. It's OK if you contracept now."

Another priest told a woman, "You have had six kids. You've done enough. You can get your tubes tied!" With these words her husband felt abandoned. Though *he* embraced Church teaching, he stood alone against their parish priest. *No* priest can authorize what the Church declares to be unauthorizable.

How can *we* live truth when priests undermine the Church's teaching? Their efforts to make life easier for a couple denies that couple the freedom that comes from living true marital sexuality. Some priests even sanction abortion under the guise of concern, while dodging their real responsibility of assisting couples through difficult or unwanted pregnancies. These dissenting clerics thwart God's plan by withholding truth. They wrongly sanction contraception, sterilization, or abortion rather than help couples truly live Church teaching in its splendor.

Confused. The Church has never been confused about marital sexual morality; some Catholics, however, are. In their confusion they mock the Church's teaching as unrealistic. Some have raised large families but then discourage their adult children from doing the same, since contraception is now readily available. They may have lived Church teaching without understanding it, and their incomplete understanding leads them to discourage their children from living it.

Some parents set a poor example by not following Church teaching on openness to life. They cannot speak to a truth they have neither understood nor lived. Still others have had sex *only* for babies, to the exclusion of healthy marriage and family life. They also fail to understand and live an essential aspect of sexual marital love.

We are bombarded by statistics claiming that most Catholics are not living the Church's teaching. This becomes adult peer pressure to do the wrong thing. As we point out to our children, that proves nothing. Since it does not suit the media's purpose to tell us, we do not hear about many *more* Christian couples living the truth of marital sexuality.

Living these truths is not easy. During a conversation with five committed Catholic women, I heard the following: "When I thought I could be pregnant, I was horrified,…

sad,…scared to death,…fearful." And, "When I found out I wasn't pregnant, I was so relieved,…grateful. It was such a blessing!"

Was this just a safe environment where they could be honest? Or as they shared conflicted feelings about love and children, was it a cry for prayer and practical help? We are to train our hearts—and others' hearts—in truth! Just as we encourage our teens to use positive peer conversation for chastity, so we need positive peer conversation among couples to encourage marital chastity.

Angry or sad. Now—too late—many people realize they were not taught the truth. The ache in their hearts is great. In the prophetic words of Pope Paul VI, "[S]exuality too is depersonalized and exploited: from being the sign, place and language of love, that is, of the gift of self and acceptance of another."[11] Many lament that selfishness, rather than a well-formed conscience, dictated their decisions, and now it is too late to conceive.

A FRESH START

We are responsible to understand why the Church teaches what she does. If we understand the truth about marital sexuality, we can become living witnesses of that truth to the next generation. We cannot change the past, but we can impact the future. Our mission is to help young people understand that *they* have a mission: responsible parenthood in Christian marriage.

CHAPTER FOUR

The Mission of Responsible Parenthood

We have limited time in which we can offer our fertility in service to God. If God's response is "Yes, now!" we know his will for this time in our lives. If his response is "Not yet," we serve him in other ways. Married love "requires in husband and wife an awareness of their mission of 'responsible parenthood.'"[1]

THE POWER OF OUR FERTILITY

Responsible parenthood begins by acknowledging the power of our fertility. God designed women so that their strongest desire for intercourse is during ovulation. That reveals part of God's intent. This is not an instinct to suppress, but a God-given desire for intimacy and unity with one's spouse that may culminate in a new life.

We embrace the power of our sexuality. "Acceptance of the possibility of procreation in the marital relationship safeguards love and is an indispensable condition of a truly personal union."[2] We make prudent decisions that reflect generous hearts toward God and each other.

Fragility of our fertility. Responsible parenthood means that we recognize the fragility of our fertility. Many couples are amazed to find that *not* contracepting does not guarantee a baby.

Consider this: Our opportunities to conceive and deliver a child are limited. In light of eternity, how long will our lives be?

In light of our lives, how many years will we be married? In light of our marriage, how many times will we conceive? And of the babies we conceive, how many will we bring to term?

Couples experience how fragile fertility is in several ways. Many couples presume they have years of fertility, so they delay having children; then they discover the window of opportunity has already closed. Some couples conceive easily at first, only to experience secondary infertility. Other couples experience miscarriage or stillbirth. When I suffered our third miscarriage, no special testing was done to find a cause, because losing three was considered normal.

Generosity of heart. Given both the power and fragility of our fertility, we are called to *responsible parenthood* in one of two ways. Couples fulfill the call "to exercise responsible parenthood who prudently and generously decide to have a large family, or who, for serious reasons and with due respect to the moral law, choose to have no more children for the time being or even for an indeterminate period."[3]

Our generosity reflects Jesus' generosity toward us. When Jesus said, "This is my body broken for you; this is my blood shed for you," he echoed Mary's self-donating love. Even before our Lord said these words, Mary enacted them in giving birth to Jesus. Likewise, every mother says this to each of her children.

Instead of thinking we control destiny, we entrust this personal, vital, intimate relationship to God. The duty "for which married persons are the free and responsible collaborators of God the Creator, has always been a source of great joys to them, even if sometimes accompanied by not a few difficulties and distress."[4]

Currently, in first-world countries, many families are only open to one or at most two children. Think of the people who have made a profound difference in history who were *not* first- or second-born in their families: Ludwig van Beethoven (fifth-born), Moses (third-born), David (the eighth son), Saint Thérèse of Lisieux (ninth-born), and Saint Catherine of Siena (twenty-fifth-born), to name only a few.

How about those around us? How many are not "premium" children (that is, first- or second-born)? And for those of us who are, how many of us have one or both parents who were not first- or second-born? (My mother is a fifth-born.) How many of us would not be here if the first two to be born were the only valuable children in a family? We need to challenge this thinking.

One husband struggled when his fourth child was expected, until I reminded him that his wife was the fourth-born of a fifth-born! That brought a note of reality and even gratitude to his thoughts.

Sibling revelry. Generosity toward God translates into generosity toward our spouse and children. We build up the family by bearing and nurturing our children, giving them the gift of siblings.

I questioned my dad when I was expecting our second child. "I know I will love this child as much as Michael, but I don't know how. I love Michael with all my heart!"

"You're thinking about love the wrong way, as if it gets divided," Dad replied. "Love is multiplied with each new family member. Not only will you have a unique love for this child, but he will bring love to each member of your family."

We need a new term: Let's replace *sibling rivalry* with *sibling revelry.* The week before our son Joseph was born, our eleven-year-old Michael approached me. "Mom, is there anything more exciting in the world than having a baby?" I smiled. What a joy to share that moment of anticipation together. Later he told me that when we called with news of Joseph's birth, he ran door-to-door throughout the neighborhood, telling everyone the news. That's sibling joy!

I had the same experience. When I was seven, Dad took my laboring mom to the hospital. I was the first to get the news: I had a new baby sister, Kristen. How could I tell the neighbors? I ran into the middle of the street and screamed at the top of my lungs, "It's a girl!" Then I went door-to-door to deliver my message personally. That's sibling delight!

When I delivered David, our sixteen-year-old son Michael drove himself and two siblings to the hospital. It was amazing to watch my eldest sons, both six feet tall, enter the room and take turns holding this precious new brother. I still had wires and tubes connecting me to my IV stand, so I was immobile.

Gabriel approached my bedside, tenderly took my hand, tears filling his eyes, and said, "How will I ever find the words to thank you?" That's sibling revelry!

NATURAL FAMILY PLANNING

What if a couple has a serious reason for delaying conception? What moral options do they have?

Periodic abstinence through Natural Family Planning (NFP) is their only moral option. Every act of marriage is to be open to life; otherwise we refuse that gift of the other. But God's design of our bodies reveals that every act cannot result in new life, since a woman's monthly cycle includes only 100 to 120 hours of fertility.[5]

Using NFP principles, married couples adhere to moral guidelines when they abstain from intercourse during times of fertility and make love during times of infertility. This is *not* your parents' *rhythm method!* The rhythm method was one formula applied to any woman, and many women did not fit the norm.

NFP helps a couple understand changes in the woman's body throughout the fertility cycle: varying temperatures, types and amounts of mucus flow, and openness of her cervix. Principles for detecting fertility pertain to an individual woman, as opposed to the one-size-fits-all approach of the rhythm method. With this information a couple decides whether or not they have a serious reason to abstain during their time of mutual fertility (assuming the man is always fertile).

Some people mistakenly think NFP is required. However, couples preferring to be open to new life are not obligated to use it.

A contracepting couple does not pay attention to signs of fertility. Either the woman mindlessly takes a contraceptive pill, puts in a diaphragm, or waits for her husband to put on a condom every time. In fact, various forms of the pill or the patch disrupt normal cycles, so that a woman's signs of fertility are altered.

NFP is *not* Catholic contraception, in which a couple feasts on love and then rejects the fruit of that love. Even when a couple misuses NFP with selfish intentions, it is not accurate to say they have a "contraceptive mentality." Contraception deliberately thwarts the life-giving capacity of marital intimacy. NFP is a choice to abstain during fertility, anticipating when you can receive each other in fruitful love.

Marital abstinence can be considered in light of Mass and the Eucharist. God, through his Church, calls us to go to Mass every Sunday. If for some reason we are unable to observe the one-hour fast before Communion, we abstain from the Eucharist. Certainly, receiving Jesus in fruitful love is best. But when we cannot, we still go to Mass, enjoy his presence, and anticipate when we will be able to receive him again.

Serious reasons. Christian couples enjoy the beauty and power of marital sexuality as part of God's plan for their marriage. "In its true meaning, responsible procreation requires couples to be obedient to the Lord's call and to act as faithful interpreters of his plan. This happens when the family is generously open to new lives, and when couples maintain an attitude of openness and service to life, even if, for serious reasons and in respect for the moral law, they choose to avoid a new birth for the time being or indefinitely."[6]

For serious reasons, which a couple discerns, a couple can use NFP to delay pregnancy. It functions similarly to a prescription for difficulty rather than the norm for marital life.

There is no standardized list of reasons for using NFP. We pray for prudent and generous hearts, and then we weigh our concerns. For example, Jesus admonishes the disciples, "Therefore do not be anxious about tomorrow, for tomorrow will be anxious for itself" (Matthew 6:34). But Saint Paul teaches, "If any one does not provide for his relatives, and especially for his own family, he has disowned the faith and is worse than an unbeliever" (1 Timothy 5:8). So we balance *trusting* God to provide for our family with *working* to provide for our family, praying for wisdom to know if our circumstance warrants NFP at this time.

We may be unsure how to divide our time, attention, love, or even financial resources for another child. Our perspective is limited but valid; we base our judgments on faith informed by reason. Though we may use NFP, we trust that should God give us another child, he will provide what we need. We want hearts ready to receive children with joy from the Lord. Entrusting our plans to him, we then discern his plan for us.

Benefits of NFP. Some people use NFP because it is a *natural* as opposed to an artificial means of delaying conception. (That is not why the Church allows NFP.) It is worth noting that there are no unpleasant or dangerous physical side effects, either for the mom or for a baby conceived. Since no doctor's assistance is required, it is an inexpensive way to regulate births even in poor countries.

NFP is better than contraception because it is a *moral* option. It involves the sacrifices of both husband and wife, based on their convictions rather than convenience. Both understand that periodic abstinence is an act of love for the beloved. And when NFP is followed carefully, it is as effective as the pill. Yes, the pill! After all, if a couple is convinced that there are serious reasons not to conceive at the present moment, would it not be better to utilize a method that is effective? Unlike contraception, NFP also yields helpful information for when a couple hopes to conceive.

We have to watch assumptions. *Planning* can imply control. When it comes to making babies, control is an illusion. We can plan when we are open to life, but we cannot plan either to make a baby or not to: Ultimately God is the one in control. God opens the womb; God closes the womb (see Genesis 30:22; 1 Samuel 1:6). Certainly a child has no less value because *we* did not plan him or her—*God did!* When we enjoy marital sexuality, we embrace the fullness of God's plan for our marriage.

Continue in tender love. Be careful that you do not treat each other as untouchable when you are fertile. Continue to express tender love. At the same time, Saint Paul cautions, "Do not refuse one another except perhaps by agreement for a season, that you may devote yourselves to prayer; but then come together again, lest Satan tempt you through lack of self-control" (1 Corinthians 7:5).

Through NFP the discipline of self-control helps couples during those times when it is inadvisable to express love physically: times of illness or injury, and when a woman is in danger of miscarriage or recovering from a delivery. We experienced this.

I hemorrhaged mid-pregnancy with Hannah. At the hospital we discovered that she was alive and well, but she had attached to my cervix, a condition known as *placenta previa*. Either sexual intercourse or labor could endanger her life by causing her umbilical cord to disconnect. The doctor told me that we would have to abstain for six months until my recovery following delivery. Six months!

Since we had already used self-control with NFP, Scott knew that, though it would be hard, it was possible to abstain. He could do what was best for our baby and me. He found ways to show me tender love throughout the pregnancy, massaging my legs, feet, and back when I was on many days of bed rest. Hannah arrived safe and sound, and our marriage even grew through that trial.

Whatever we do we need to do *in faith:* being open to life or being open to life while using NFP. Let's live the truth of God's beautiful design for marriage.

CHAPTER FIVE

Answering the Critics

L et's briefly examine arguments for contraception that you may hear from parents, siblings, friends, or coworkers. We want to be able to address their concerns.

Contraception seems reasonable.

Objection: When a couple waits until marriage to have sex, why should they abstain during marriage? Contraception enables a couple to have sex whenever they want.

Response: Ultimately we are motivated by what is best for our spouse. We respect the integrity of our marital intimacy, not separating the unitive and procreative purposes of lovemaking. Most of our married life we will be able to make love when we choose. If we discern a serious reason not to conceive, we can observe periodic abstinence during our fertile time. Our self-control before marriage helps us to have self-control during marriage. Self-control is both an act of will, as we cherish our beloved, and a fruit of the Spirit, which fosters our spiritual growth.

Contraception seems logical.

Objection: Women do not have to be ruled by hormonal desires for a baby. Using rational thoughts, they can suppress longings for children. Unlike animals, who copulate according to instinct, humans can use reason and then use contraceptives.

Response: Most animals, ruled by instinct, only copulate when the female is in heat. As human beings, we are not ruled by instinct. Regardless of where we are in our fertility cycle, we can enjoy interpersonal communion in our marital sexuality. A woman's desire for her spouse during ovulation is not an instinct to suppress but a God-given desire for expressing life-giving love. We *can* and should use free will to make decisions about our family, but it has to be done in love, for love. The act of marriage, unfettered by contraceptives, is a complete gift of self and a rational act of obedience.

It sounds intelligent to use contraception.

Objection: Before the availability of modern birth control, couples did not have options. We have developed technology that can control our fertility, rather than have fertility control us. Should we ignore it?

Response: There is no moral imperative to use technology if it is immoral, such as embryonic stem cell research or cloning. The prior question to ask is, does this technology help you understand creation better (like exploring space or oceans) or counter the effects of sin (like curing diseases)?

Contraception does not help you understand your body better. It is put in or on your body, regardless of where a woman is in her fertility cycle. Contraception does not heal and frequently causes harm. Fertility is not a disease to be controlled.

The pill treats fertility more like an illness than a natural good. Common complaints about the pill include weight gain, irritability, decreased sex drive, and even depression. Despite contraceptive ads' soothing music, beautiful scenery, and gentle voices, these ads acknowledge terrible physical consequences for women. Side effects include increased chance of heart attack, stroke, blood clots, and infertility.[1] Should this be the role of medicine—to cause well-functioning organs to malfunction?

At a time when our society discourages drugs, why would men insist women use contraceptive drugs? Does this express love? What message does this give young women, especially when their own mothers are the ones providing the pills?

The most serious consequence of the pill is its action as an abortifacient. When I was preparing for marriage, my OB/GYN offered me the mini-pill. I was not yet Catholic, and his offer seemed reasonable. I asked about possible side effects. "None to speak of," he responded. I would have known differently had I read the tiny print under "Possible Side Effects," but I wanted the easy solution the doctor was offering.

Immediately this little pill altered my clockwork-like cycle. Five weeks before my wedding day, a scant three weeks from my last cycle, I had a period. That was odd. Two weeks later I had another period, which ended the day after my wedding. That was frustrating. At the end of our ten-day honeymoon, I began another period! That was unendurable! Do you know anyone who had not one but two periods on their honeymoon? Something was very wrong.

I was only home briefly to pack for our major move. My doctor was in Europe, but his assistant suggested that I double the dose and see a doctor after our move.

I followed his instructions and had no period for ten weeks. Was I pregnant? I called a doctor for an appointment.

Though the pregnancy test was negative, the doctor told me something no one had yet told me. The mini-pill I was taking was potentially abortive. It did not suppress ovulation; it only damaged the lining of my uterus so that a baby could not implant.

I stopped taking the mini-pill immediately. When I shared this information with Scott, he agreed that we would switch to barrier methods only. I later discovered that even the regular pill does not always suppress ovulation. When breakthrough ovulation occurs, the dual action of damaging uterine lining to prevent implantation can cause an abortion too, just as an I.U.D. can.

That fall I gave a number of talks on abortion and was surprised at how often questions about contraception emerged. I was intrigued. Was contraception a moral issue? My study in a class on Christian ethics led Scott and me to change our minds and our practice. We switched to NFP to delay conception for a few months and then used the information to try to get pregnant.

Contraception seems responsible.

Objection: With contraception we limit our family size or have a child-free marriage, so we do not contribute to societal difficulties that come with children. We can plan the number and spacing of children and fit them into our financial or career plans.

Response: Responsible parenthood does not reduce a child to an object to acquire nor a problem to avoid. Responsible parenthood recognizes both the power of marital sexuality *and* the gift of a child. When there are serious reasons to not conceive, a couple has access to NFP.

Too many couples feel constrained to prove to others that they have planned their pregnancy. They delay a baby until it fits their overall financial, social, or career plans. They feel they must justify the timing and spacing for each birth *and* the reason they have not yet stopped having children. People they barely know candidly question them: "Did you plan this baby?" Or, "Now that you have a boy and a girl, are you done?"

Some ask, "Don't you understand what causes this?" Others might confront a husband as they did a friend: "Can't you keep your hands off your wife?" They may think your openness to life exhibits a flagrant disregard for the well-being of others.

Most people know that others' financial affairs are not to be questioned publicly, if at all. In polite society one does not ask, "How can you afford that appliance, those house payments, or college tuition?" Yet the same ones barge into our bedrooms by questioning our openness to life, asking, "Can you afford all of these children?" They must not realize how inappropriate their probing is.

Should someone feel compelled to recommend a good doctor to *fix* you, summon the courage to tell them that nothing is broken. Let them know they are insulting your intelligence and faith. Dr. Janet Smith, professor of moral theology at Sacred Heart Seminary, writes, "Many in our culture cannot imagine life without contraception. They think the alternative means no sexual intercourse at all or lots of babies. Since our culture is so obsessed with sex and so hostile to babies, both possibilities seem unthinkable."[2]

Contraception seems like common sense.

Objection: Instead of satisfying a selfish desire for more children, why not help needy people? In fact, maybe you should help needy people not have children, so they will not be so poor. Sterilizations are cheaper than paying for children on welfare.

Response: This is a false dilemma. Responsible sexuality in our own marriage is a separate issue from our care for the poor.

Responsible sexuality means we apply our ability to reason and to control our desires with our will toward the greatest good. Frankly, the more children we have, the more people there will be to help care for the poor in the future, since we intend to raise them as compassionate persons of faith.

Our children will be problem solvers—givers, not takers, in our society. They will offer care that does not include discouraging poor people from the blessing of children. Have you noticed how many impoverished people value their children over possessions? They know that life does not consist in things but in love shared in families.

In the early 1970s a friend in Boston went for a walk. She held the hands of her three-year-old and two-year-old, had a one-year-old in a backpack, and was noticeably pregnant with her next child. A man approached and spit on her, saying, "It's people like you causing all the problems in this world!"

If it had been me, I would probably have spit back. But my friend was gracious. She simply replied, "I don't know how you can look at these precious children and think they are the problem!"

In the midst of our riches in the United States, are we capable of seeing the poverty of devaluing life?

CULTURAL CONSEQUENCES OF CONTRACEPTION

The child is devalued. Contraception attacks the fruit of love. It promotes sterility rather than fertility. When contraception "fails," a child becomes the problem for which abortion may be the fall-back solution.

Instead we embrace life in the midst of a culture war between life and death. God creates and sustains life. Satan is anti-life, literally contra-*ceptus!* He cannot create; he can only destroy.

A Protestant woman was picketing Planned Parenthood for promoting abortions. Suddenly she realized that she used contraceptive products that Planned Parenthood promoted. "No more!" she told me. "We need to be more than *anti-abortion*; we need to be *pro-life!*"

Sometimes children grasp this more readily than we do. I was talking with our son Joe, ten at the time, when he asked, "Could you have killed me?"

His question took my breath away. "No!" I responded immediately.

"But *could* you have killed me?"

I responded, "Yes, Joe, legally I could have, but I never would have."

I realized in a moment the horror of the reality of abortion for our children. Each child born since *Roe* v. *Wade* legalized abortion on January 22, 1973, is an abortion holocaust survivor. Someone had to decide *not* to kill them! That reality pierced my heart. I hope someday there will be an Abortion Holocaust Survivors' March.

I was in high school the year after abortion was legalized. I was with a friend when, in an outburst of anger, her mother blurted, "It's a good thing abortion wasn't legal when I was expecting you, or you wouldn't be here!"

I could hardly breathe! How could a mother let herself think, let alone say, something so cruel to her child? Other parents lament how their life changed because of their child. "If you hadn't come, I could have done this with my education, or had that career…. If not for you, I wouldn't have married your dad…." What does a child do with such thoughtless and unkind comments? Words can exact a terrible price, leaving scars that last a lifetime.

We see devastating effects as "quality of life" rather than "value of life" ethics become the norm. Some Americans have opened the door to infanticide by denying medical assistance to babies surviving abortion and to euthanasia by allowing assisted suicide (now legal in Oregon and Washington). These are among the dangers Pope Paul VI clearly warned us about with his promulgation of *Humanae Vitae* in 1968.

Woman is devalued. Contraception is contrary to the integrity of the act of marriage and the dignity of the human persons involved. Pope Paul VI wrote, "Another effect that gives cause for alarm is that a man who grows accustomed to the use of contraceptive methods may forget the reverence due to a woman, and, disregarding her physical and emotional equilibrium, reduce her to a mere instrument for the satisfaction of his own desires."[3]

Contraception allows people to use each other.
Initially many ridiculed Pope Paul VI's warnings, but his words have proven prophetic. Contraceptive use has enabled many unmarried women to fall into the trap of using sex to feel loved. And it has enabled men and women to engage in infidelity more freely. For married women it has increased the pressure to perform or be set aside for someone new. And some countries even have stripped women of their right to bear their own children. "Sterilization is forced on unsuspecting women in third world countries, with China's one-child-per-couple policy in the vanguard."[4]

Marriage is devalued. The culture of death surrounding us has had a deeper impact on our collective American psyche than we realize. Not only does our culture reject unborn children, but it devalues marriage. People are reduced to objects. And what do we do with objects? We collect them, use them, shelve them, and throw them away. What do we do with people we treat as objects? Use them and throw them away.

No-fault divorce has encouraged couples to split rather than do the difficult work of restoring their marriage. Taxpayers who cohabit get better tax breaks than at least 40 percent of married couples.[5] Tax funds subsidize Planned Parenthood, the single largest abortion provider in the United States. They, in turn, help schoolchildren acquire contraceptives without parental knowledge or consent. Some states have even redefined marriage.

Many families have fewer aunts, uncles, cousins, and siblings due to contraceptive use. Child counselors are seeing children who are experiencing deep loneliness and depression, sensitive to the loss of these family members. In fact, contraception's consequences have had a generational force, as whole bloodlines have been choked off.

This is the society in which we live. How do we catch a different vision for marriage and family life? We train our hearts in the truths that can transform our thinking. By God's grace we can nurture a culture of love and life, beginning with our own family.

Chapter Six

Training Our Hearts in Truth

We train our hearts in truth, reflecting on the privilege of imaging God's love by giving life. Jesus said, "Greater love has no man than this, that a man lay down his life for his friends" (John 15:13). Every delivery is an opportunity for a woman to lay down her life for her child, though death in childbirth is rare.

Gianna Beretta Molla was an Italian pediatrician, wife, and mother. In September 1961 Gianna's doctor diagnosed a serious uterine fibroma that had to be removed, but she was in the second month of her fourth pregnancy. The doctor recommended an abortion to save her life. Fully understanding the medical risk, Gianna chose to save the baby instead. She gave birth to her daughter, Gianna Emanuela, and died one week later from septic peritonitis. "Saint Gianna Beretta Molla, protectress of mothers and families, died in 1962, as a martyr of maternal love."[1]

> A woman of exceptional love, an outstanding wife and mother, she gave witness in her daily life to the demanding values of the Gospel. By holding up this woman as an exemplar of Christian perfection, we would like to extol all those high-spirited mothers of families who give themselves completely to their family, who suffer in giving birth, who are prepared for every labor and every kind of sacrifice, so that the best they have can be given to others.[2]

Saint Gianna is a model of life-giving love for all of us.

THE VALUE OF SUFFERING

Saint Paul reveals the value of suffering that is united to Christ's. "Now I rejoice in my sufferings for your sake, and in my flesh I complete what is lacking in Christ's afflictions for the sake of his body, that is, the Church" (Colossians 1:24). In my pregnancies and deliveries as a Catholic, I consciously united my suffering to Christ's self-offering. It did not hurt less (I thought it might), but it was more meaningful. I offered up the indignities of nakedness in front of strangers, laid out cruciform as they prepared me for another C-section, pricked with needles, shaking from a cold operating room, and in pain.

In parenting we have many smaller sacrifices to make. Do we prefer "nails" in front of others to "pinpricks" no one sees? Do we consider making passive offerings: no creamer in our coffee or sugar in our tea or declining second servings? We can list the tasks we have to do that day alongside our prayer concerns. Then we can offer something for each task, with joy. Saint Josemaría Escrivá says, "For by the constant practice of repeated self-denial in little things, with God's grace you will increase in strength and manliness of character."[3] We also need to be mindful to "choose mortifications that don't mortify others."[4]

Hope for the future: dealing with—miscarriage. When your womb becomes a tomb, you have many questions for which there may not be answers. You may have physical pain; you have emotional pain. In miscarriage or stillbirth, you experience a death of dreams individually, as a couple, and as a family. It is an intensely personal loss, no matter how common such losses may be. It feels especially painful when you long for new life while others are casting off their young through abortion.

My sister Kari has been pregnant fifteen times: She has lost eight babies in miscarriage and has raised seven with her husband, Mark. We have shared joy at the news of pregnancy and tender times of sadness in shared loss.

Recently Kari recounted what occurred when she was caring for her dying grandmother-in-law. Kari noticed the elderly woman's smile, as if she were looking at someone. Kari asked, "What do you see, Mamaw?"

"Six little girls around my bed." They were alone in the room.

A few hours later Kari ventured a follow-up question. "Mamaw, what did the little girls look like?"

"I don't think I should tell you."

"It's OK, Mamaw. What did they look like?"

"They looked like Molly." Molly is one of Kari's daughters. Could six of the eight babies she miscarried be girls? God knows, but Mamaw seemed to see a reality beyond the limits of time and space.

Scott and I have miscarried three babies. We found it comforting to name them: Raphael, Noel Francis, and Angelica Frances. When Kari and I shared about our losses, she said, "It's like storing treasure in heaven."

We cannot take anything with us when we die, but we can send a bit of ourselves ahead if our children precede us in death. If the goal of Christian parenting is heaven, we have already succeeded with those children who have died. And I believe we are different parents because of their love and prayers on our behalf.

A couple mailed a birth announcement of their son who died just after birth. They expressed their faith in the midst of great suffering, quoting Romans 11:33–36. Above their son's picture they wrote this heartbreakingly beautiful phrase, "Heaven announces the birth of their newest arrival...."

If someone you know has lost a child, acknowledge their loss. Do not be afraid to weep with those who weep. Your compassion and love are needed. For practical suggestions following a miscarriage or stillbirth, see my book *Life-Giving Love*, chapter ten (Servant, 2002).

Hope for the future: dealing with—infertility. Growing numbers of couples in the United States, approximately 10 percent of those in their childbearing years, are struggling with primary or secondary infertility. According to the American Society for Reproductive Medicine, that is "more than 6 million American women and their spouses."[5]

When you are married, it is never selfish to pray for a baby. It is the right request in the right relationship. However, "marriage does not confer upon the spouses the right to have a child, but only the right to perform those natural acts which are *per se* ordered to procreation."[6] That is why some actions to resolve infertility are moral and others are not. The goal is not a child at any price.

The pain of infertility increases when people misunderstand your private agony and probe with questions. Strangers may "hint" that it is time to start your family. You wonder if you have to announce publicly your private pain, so not to be misjudged. Or should you suffer silently and tolerate being misunderstood? Well meaning or not, others' lack of tact makes the pain of infertility more intense.

Ask our Lord to protect your heart from despair while you sort through various disappointments and difficulties. Ask him to keep you and your spouse close during a time that could pull you apart. Try not to reduce lovemaking to baby-making: You add pressure and risk the possibility that one or both of you could feel used. As one woman wrote, "I'm trying to let go of the intensity of my desire without despairing that it may not be fulfilled."

At the same time, explore all moral options. In *Life-Giving Love*, chapter eleven, I explain procedures that are in line with Church teaching and why some procedures are not licit. The Pope Paul VI Institute has helped many couples conceive.[7] The people there are committed to offering procedures the Church allows.

When you feel as if the pain is too great even to articulate a prayer, let the Holy Spirit pray *for* you. Saint Paul reminds us, "Likewise the Spirit helps us in our weakness; for we do not know how to pray as we ought, but the Spirit himself intercedes for us with sighs too deep for words" (Romans 8:26).

FUNDAMENTAL CONFLICT OF MINDSETS

There is conflict between the mind of God and the mind-set of this world. How can we resist conforming to lies regarding what it is to be a man or a woman? What constitutes a marriage? What is the value of a child? Is the marriage bond indissoluble? What is the meaning of marital sexuality?

The world says, what will serve *you* the most?

And God says, what will serve *me* the most?

The world says, you can get married without intending to share your life with children. But if you do intend to have kids, first consider whether a child is an economic liability or interferes with your education and career.

The Lord says, children are the supreme gift of marriage because they reveal the life-giving power of love.

The world says, if you are going to have children, limit it to one or two children, and then get sterilized to keep your "all-American" family.

The Lord says, the generosity expressed in a large family shows great blessing. Even if you think you should not have more children, never mutilate a part of your body so that you can never again use it for me.

The world says, if you have experienced the pain of miscarriage or stillbirth, avoid being open to life. No need to subject yourself to senseless suffering.

The Lord says, any child you have lost in death still lives for all eternity with me. Suffering offered to me is never meaningless.

The world says, look at what a good Catholic you are. You agree with so much that the Church says. On average you are certainly better than most.

The Lord says, it is not about how much you agree with the Church but about how much you yield your heart, mind, will, and body to me. A cafeteria Catholic, who picks and chooses what is palatable in Church teaching, is not truly Catholic. Remember my words: "Not every one who says to me, 'Lord, Lord,' shall enter the kingdom of heaven, but he who does the will of my Father who is in heaven" (Matthew 7:21).

WHAT DOES IT TAKE TO LIVE THIS VISION?
It takes faith, hope, and love to live this vision.

We need *faith* to respond to God's call. We do not know the future, but we know the One who does, and we place our trust in him (see James 4:13–16). We approach him boldly, as a child approaches his father. "Let us then with confidence draw near to the throne of grace, that we may receive mercy and find grace to help in time of need" (Hebrews 4:16). We receive grace when we need it, not before. (We do not need grace for a fifth child unless we already have four.) "My God will supply every need of yours according to his riches in glory in Christ Jesus" (Philippians 4:19).

We need *hope* to believe God's vision for building the kingdom, one person at a time, through us. "We know that in everything God works for good with those who love him, who are called according to his purpose" (Romans 8:28). Everything! There is no such thing as purposeless suffering, though the purposes may unfold gradually, and we may not understand them this side of heaven.

We need *love* to imitate Christ's sacrificial self-offering. "I have been crucified with Christ; it is no longer I who live, but Christ who lives in me; and the life I now live in the flesh I live by faith in the Son of God, who loved me and gave himself for me" (Galatians 2:20).

Is it difficult to carry the cross? Yes; it is a *cross.* But we do not carry it alone.

Support from the body of Christ. The body of Christ reflects God's love in practical ways. This is why we make our wedding vows in front of witnesses: We need accountability and assistance. "Bear one another's burdens, and so fulfil the law of Christ" (Galatians 6:2). We need hearts open to the Lord and to our spouse. As couples we should assist other couples so they can keep their hearts open as well.

Children are not the burden. The other stuff is: extra laundry, less time to clean, fatigue, nausea…. We offer practical help so that young families feel supported, fulfilling Saint Paul's command for older women to teach younger women how to love their children and husbands (see Titus 2:3–5). His goal, and ours, is that the gospel is not discredited. "We who are strong ought to bear with the failings of the weak" (Romans 15:1a). We can assist young families to embrace God's beautiful design for marriage.[8]

Priests, in particular, can offer counseling and spiritual guidance to married couples. Priests truly father couples into greater wholeness *and* holiness by faithfully teaching truth, offering encouragement, and making the sacraments available.

Lessons learned from my "littles." What have I learned from the pregnancies with my little ones?

With Michael I learned that a baby is always worth the *wait*. We tried to get pregnant for nine months before we conceived him. Then we had to wait fifteen days past the due date for his delivery.

With Gabriel I learned how to plead for a child's life while bleeding during pregnancy. I witnessed the importance of insisting a doctor prove that my child was dead before following her advice to "come in and get cleaned out." The ultrasound, which showed Gabriel leaping and dancing, saved his life. I never set foot in that doctor's office again.

With Hannah, as we rushed to the hospital with blood running down my leg, I learned to thank God for the four and a half months I had already had with my child. Scott and I prayed for her life and wept as we saw her still alive on the ultrasound. Periodic bed rest for *placenta previa*, early (dangerous) labor, and a planned C-section taught me to relinquish control over my life.

With our miscarriages of Raphael (who died January 22, 1989) and Noel Francis (who died December 18, 1989), I learned not to take the birth of a child for granted. I chose to celebrate each child for as long as we had him or her and to rejoice that he or she would exist for all eternity.

Following those two miscarriages I conceived Jeremiah. As I shared earlier, I learned through his pregnancy to give my fears of loss to God. I prayed, trusting him with my life and my baby's. Still yielding to God's will, I asked that I might have the privilege of raising him.

With Angelica Frances (who died October 3, 1993), I learned how joy multiplies when we share about our new baby with our children. Then I learned how sorrows are lessened when our children help us to bear the loss of a child.

With Joseph I learned that God sometimes surprises you with a child you did not believe you could conceive. One day Joseph and I were talking in the kitchen, and all of a sudden he asked, "How soon did the baby die before you conceived me?"

"Joseph, I miscarried just weeks before we conceived you."

"So if that baby had not died, I wouldn't be here, would I?"

"No, Joseph."

Joseph thought for a moment, and he shared this profound thought: "Mom, I'm sorry the other baby died, but this way you get to have us both!"

What an amazing thought!

With David I learned that even a forty-one-year-old body can produce a beautiful baby. I felt that I was old; God obviously did not. When David was two days old, I wrote in my prayer journal, "I feel like this whole experience has been a wonderful expression of love between Scott and me, to live the Church's teachings more deeply in front of our children. It's been great to take on the sacrifices—and to share the joy."

Recently David announced, "There has to be one more baby in there!" I felt his anguish when I told him that, though we were open, God was probably saying my body was too old. Through David I am learning the sadness of being the last child but also the beauty of being a young uncle who relishes time with his nieces.

What have you learned from your children? How has God used their sweet dependence on you for life itself to reveal your dependence on God? We have so much to learn from them and with them.

RESPECT THE SANCTITY OF MARRIAGE

Through our sacraments of baptism and holy matrimony, we are consecrated for our vocation—blessed to be a blessing. Through faithfulness to the Lord and to each other, the communion between spouses becomes the wellspring for a community of persons. Through us God creates a civilization of love within our family. And then through our families, he touches the world.

We embrace marital chastity, willing to develop self-mastery. Self-mastery transforms our love and strengthens us to face our responsibilities with tranquility. Then we can witness to the joys and sacrifices of family life. Difficulties exist, but the solution is not contraception or sterilization; the solution is prayer and the grace of the sacraments.

Embrace a new beginning. Right now can be a new beginning! If you are using contraception, you can decide that you will no longer participate in contraceptive sex. By God's grace, through the sacrament of reconciliation, you and your spouse can be set free to live the truth of marital sexuality. Discern with a priest how much culpability you have had. Receive grace to live the life to which you have been called.

If you or your spouse has been sterilized, go to confession with a priest who will help you determine your culpability. Neither you nor your spouse is required to reverse the procedure. However, many couples who have had reversals testify to how free they now feel, having undone the damage they caused. See *Life-Giving Love*, chapter twelve, for information specific to the issue of sterilization.

A new freedom. Let's ask the Lord to renew our minds and form our consciences with truths that transform. And let's deepen our desire to be generous with time, talents, treasure, and even our bodies in faithfulness to our vocation.

We have the grace *to see, understand,* and *commit our lives,* marriages, and families *to truth.* Jesus said, "If you continue in my word, you are truly my disciples, and you will know the truth, and the truth will make you free" (John 8:31b–32). This is true freedom!

PART THREE

She Makes

Linen Garments

and Sells Them

CHAPTER SEVEN

Facing the Financial Future Without Fear

When my sons were little, I attended a luncheon for mothers, most of whom were home full-time. The speaker was a young mother and a full-time OB/GYN with on-call hours to deliver babies. She shared quality conversations she had with her children. She challenged the idea of a quantity of time when quality time was possible. Then she cautioned us, "It's important to be known as something more than 'Johnny's mom.'"

I looked around my table; every woman was nodding. I wanted to interrupt: "Doesn't that depend on who Johnny is? Saint John the Baptist? Saint John Chrysostom? John Calvin? President John F. Kennedy? Pope John Paul II? And might not who he is depend on what I do to help Johnny be who he will be?"

Of course, our identity should not be so wrapped up in our children that we have no identity apart from them. However, our sacrifices provide the emotional capital on which their success can be built. We offer the consistent and intimate relationship our young children need so that in adulthood they can risk intimate relationships.

PRESSURES TO WORK OUTSIDE THE HOME

A young widow with four small children was urged by a friend to focus on a career that could be meaningful. She replied, "I'm going to work to protect an endangered species."

"Great! Which one?"

"Stay-at-home mothers!"

Many women feel pressured to work outside the home, even when they have small children. Family, friends, and colleagues may not value their desire to stay at home. Why live a sacrificial life of homemaking when they could pay someone else for child care? Yet Pope John Paul II said, "The 'toil' of a woman who, having given birth to a child, nourishes and cares for that child and devotes herself to its upbringing, particularly in the early years, is so great as to be comparable to any professional work."[1]

Some husbands assume two incomes are necessary. Short-term financial benefits can overshadow long-term advantages of the mother's being home. These men know that two salaries will provide stylish clothes, a bigger home, a nicer car, and a better vacation for the family. They may not understand the difficulties, psychological and emotional, their wives would have in leaving their little ones in someone else's care.

Without support many mothers hesitate to share their concerns. They may be unsure that their children will be safe, healthy, and happy in child care, especially given the high rate of turnover among day-care workers. They wonder what tender or teachable moments they will miss. They question whether they will be able to continue to breast-feed. They feel uncertain about their options should their children get sick.

On the other hand, some women are concerned that a break from their career will prevent them from reentering the work force to help with their children's college expenses. This is a valid concern; however, many women have updated their skills and reentered the work force once their children were grown. Some women assist their husbands on a farm or in a family-run business.

The critical question remains, what is best for our family now? As Brenda Hunter, author of *Home by Choice*, says, "What is central is that we fit the demands of our work around the needs of our families and not that we mortgage our children's emotional health for a career."[2]

Many wives work full-time outside the home and come home to a full-time job. They cope with internal pressure to be excellent at work and at parenting. One or both suffer. Supermom really does not exist.

Some couples or single parents are heartbroken that, with finances so tight, Mom must work outside the home. Can extended family members assist to make ends meet, either through a financial gift or by opening their home temporarily? Can landlords offer reduced rent, so that a couple could pay down debt? Might a parish offer financial counseling, money-saving ideas, or practical assistance? When offered assistance and encouragement, many more mothers, especially those of young children, might choose to be home.

THE WITNESS OF WOMEN

When you are first home with a newborn, it is a challenge to manage your time well. You may be used to a schedule imposed on you by classes or work. When you had free time, you could use it as you wished. With a newborn you have more freedom to do what is important to you but less free time to do whatever you would like.

Being home full-time is a 24/7 job, and it can be tough to not have time "off." You have less discretionary cash, which may mean fewer nice clothes, meals out, haircuts, or styling. You have less free time for hobbies and exercise. Days can feel long—and the nights short—without much of a feeling of accomplishment. And this can result in a loss of a sense of who you are. If you feel empty, poured out like a liquid offering, ask Jesus to fill you.

Can you share your struggles with your spouse so that he can help you adjust? Are there older mothers you know who could mentor you through these challenges?

Here are some stress busters I used: increase light; decrease clutter; take a nap; breathe deeply; identify the toughest time of the day and change something; journal; get some fresh air; listen to Christian or classical music; laugh; give thanks.

Cardinal Joseph Mindszenty wrote this beautiful description of a mother:

> Mother
> The Most Important Person on earth is a mother.
> She cannot claim the honor of having built Notre Dame
>   Cathedral.
> She need not.
> She has built something more magnificent than any
>   cathedral—
> a dwelling for an immortal soul, the tiny perfection of her
>   baby's body....
> The angels have not been blessed with such a grace.
> They cannot share in God's creative miracle to bring new
>   saints to Heaven.

Only a human mother can.

Mothers are closer to God the Creator than any other
creature;

God joins forces with mothers in performing this act of
creation....

What on God's good earth is more glorious than this: to
be a mother?[3]

Through correspondence and conversations, many women contributed reasons why they are grateful to be home with their children. These are helpful reminders:

PHYSICAL HEALTH

1. Child has less exposure to germs, so family is healthier.
2. Mom cares for a premature or sick child without worrying about missing work or leaving the child.
3. Mom makes home-cooked, nutritious meals.
4. Mom has time to walk with friends, with babies in strollers.

PSYCHOLOGICAL HEALTH

1. Less stress, since Mom is not hurrying her child to follow her schedule.
2. Mom's energy is focused on the priorities of family life.
3. More peace: Dad knows Mom is meeting their children's needs promptly in a nurturing environment.
4. No concern about picking up a child late from day care because of an extended workday.
5. Mom takes care of tasks during the day that are difficult when working full-time, like scheduling repairs at home, getting cars fixed, and so on.

6. Parents who were day-care or latchkey children may want their children to have a different experience.

7. Life is short, and our children are only young once. Mom can look back without regret.

FINANCIAL HEALTH

1. Fewer clothing, accessories, and makeup expenses: Less dry cleaning. Smaller wardrobe kept well.

2. No expensive lunches out.

3. No office Christmas gifts.

4. No child care costs; fewer baby-sitting costs, with play-dates with other moms from church, the neighborhood, or a baby-sitting cooperative.

5. More time to shop for sales, use coupons, and yard sale.

6. Fewer transportation costs: gas, bus, or train fares, tolls, parking.

7. Fewer car repairs: less wear and tear on car.

8. Fewer medical bills because children are sick less.

9. Mom saves money by making baby food, washing cloth diapers, and refurbishing baby furniture.

10. More time to make gifts, sew clothes, or garden.

11. More time to clean and to decorate the home—paint, wallpaper.

12. More time to pay bills and figure taxes.

13. More children are not much greater expense if Mom is home already.

14. Children do not need "things" as much as love, time, attention, and guidance.

FLEXIBLE SCHEDULE

1. More time to help children with homework, school projects, parties, and field trips.
2. More time to involve children in charitable acts: visiting the sick, making meals for others, volunteering.
3. More time to do fun things with the children.
4. Mom can monitor playmates and know children's friends better.

BETTER FOR EDUCATION OF THE CHILD

1. Children have larger vocabularies with more one-on-one conversations.
2. Mom can take children to museums and the library.
3. Mom knows she is the primary influence on her children. She communicates her values and ideals.

These are benefits that cannot be bought.

MAKING A DIFFERENCE IN THE HOME

One of my husband's students visited our home when our firstborn was six months old.

"Aren't you frustrated being home all day, not doing anything significant?"

I smiled. "Do you know what I do? I change culture, diaper by diaper!"

There is a reason for the perennial saying, "The hand that rocks the cradle rules the world." We mothers have our sphere of influence. We are doing the most important work in the world: caring for the souls and the bodies of our children.

Yet where are so many of the young mothers? One grandmother observed, "You know there's something wrong when you see more people walking dogs in the park than mothers pushing strollers."

G.K. Chesterton wrote, "How can it be a large career to tell other people's children about the Rule of Three,[4] and a small career to tell one's own children about the universe? How can it be broad to be the same thing to everyone, and narrow to be everything to someone?"[5] To have a significant influence in a child's life involves many sacrifices.

Home-centered contribution. How does the Proverbs 31 woman contribute to her family's finances? She prudently and profitably manages her time, talents, and resources. She produces marketable materials through home-working: "She perceives that her merchandise is profitable" (Proverbs 31:18a). She is a shrewd seller who "tastes" the sweet fruit of success; literally, she uses the proceeds to purchase other products for her family, like grapes or wine.

She "rises while it is yet night," and "her lamp does not go out at night" (Proverbs 31:15a, 18b). Does this woman sleep? Every mortal does. Sleep is a necessity, not a luxury. She gets the sleep she needs but without indulging in laziness.

There are three possible interpretations regarding the lamp of verse 18. First, the woman uses time wisely. Work extends beyond daylight because of her oil lamp, as for us with electricity. Evening productivity is possible given that there are fewer interruptions at that time from friends, neighbors, and young children.

Second, the woman demonstrates oversight of the home, ready to serve, like the servants in the parable who kept their loins girded and their lamps burning (see Luke 12:35–40). Jesus said that those who kept their wicks trimmed were good and faithful servants, ready to serve the master of the house.

Third, the woman might keep an oil lamp burning as a symbol of steadfastness through the darkness of sorrow, trouble, and privation. In pioneer America, when someone was expected at night, a lit candle shone in the window to guide and welcome that traveler.

Household needs come first. The Proverbs 31 woman is industrious. "She puts her hands to the distaff, and her hands hold the spindle" (verse 19). Her skill in spinning flax or wool into thread enables her to make clothes for her household. Her industry helps prepare her family for the future.

"She is not afraid of snow for her household, for all her household are clothed in scarlet" (verse 21). *Snow* refers to dangers, disasters, or difficulties. She faces these difficulties without fear. Why? She remembers God's provision for her family in the past; he is providing for her family now. She can trust him to provide for her family's future needs.

She makes clothing for herself and her family that is both attractive and protective. *Scarlet* may refer to a rich color worn by wealthy people. More likely it refers to a double layer of wool for warmth, similar to long johns worn under slacks.

"She makes herself coverings" (verse 22a). "Coverings" could include various woven items besides clothing: tapestries, rugs, cushions, tablecloths, bedspreads, quilts, and upholstery. The beauty of her home decor reflects the refreshing beauty of the Israelites' tabernacle as they wandered in the dull, dry desert.

Usually one generation instructs the next in handcrafts: how to sew, quilt, knit, crochet, and so on. Much can be lost if we are too busy to learn a handcraft from an older woman. Hopefully we will learn crafts that we can teach others.

"Her clothing is fine linen and purple" (verse 22b). She creates her own clothing that is beautiful without being ostentatious. She wears clothing fit for her station in life.

Her fabric is reminiscent of the priests' fine linen garments (see Leviticus 6:10) and the fabric worn by the bride of Christ: "'Let us rejoice and exult and give him the glory, for the marriage of the Lamb has come, and his Bride has made herself ready, it was granted her to be clothed with fine linen, bright and pure'—for the fine linen is the righteous deeds of the saints" (Revelation 19:7–8). Our good works are the fine linen covering Christ's bride.

She also wears purple, the color of nobility. When Daniel was elevated to be the third highest ruler in Belshazzar's kingdom, he was "clothed in purple" (Daniel 5:29). And when Mordecai, Queen Esther's uncle, became the Persian king's right-hand man, he left the court in "a mantle of fine linen and purple" (Esther 8:15).

"She makes linen garments and sells them; she delivers sashes to the merchant" (verse 24). She meets her household's needs before she creates sales items. (Launching a home business may not be the "order of business" for a woman with very young children.) In her home business her linen garments could be sashes or clothing.

This is home-working: hardworking, industrious labor. The point is not that the woman is working but that she is working *from home*. She cares for her children *and* makes clothing for sale.

Today there are more opportunities for home businesses than fifty years ago. This is worth considering, especially if a home business could make it possible for Mom to be home.

THE VALUE OF YOUR PRESENCE

We have an apostolate of presence in our home. We want to develop meaningful relationships with each family member, to treasure our time with each one. One new mom wrote about her baby, "I am totally, hopelessly in love with him. I want to remember every moment, every detail, yet I already realize these times that I so carefully cherish will be harder and harder to recall. For now I am content to keep the rest of the world at bay, to learn his ways, and all the ways I love him and his presence in our life."

This simple poem came to me as I pondered the wonder of my first grandchild, Veronica Margaret, and the goodness of God through my precious daughter-in-law, Sarah. I was reminded of my love for my children, for my mom, and for Mother Mary:

> Layers of Life-Nurturing Love
> I need my mother!
> Her eyes' tender gaze—not for anything I have done
>   but simply for who I am.
> Her hands' tender touch—compassion expressed for the
>   little hurts that overwhelm me,
>   though she knows how little they are.
> Her voice speaking words of love over me,
>   whether or not I understand what she is saying.
> Her breasts combining milk I need with the milk of

human kindness,
   not just giving me better food but giving me herself.
Her time, unhurried,
   as we bask in the warmth of faithful and fruitful love.
Her prayers enveloping me in the love of God,
   so that he is the air I breathe, the atmosphere of our
   home.
Her being, laid down for me,
   so that I have life and I live!
I need my mother!
Nana

Nursing. We experience the ministry of presence in a beautiful way through breast-feeding. Our bodies are stamped to the very core of our being with our calling: Our breasts produce the milk to sustain our children's lives. While he was addressing scientists in England regarding nursing, Pope John Paul II said:

> In normal circumstances these [advantages of breast-feeding] include two major benefits to the child: protection against disease and proper nourishment. Moreover, in addition to these immunological and nutritional effects, this natural way of feeding can create a bond of love and security between mother and child, and enable the child to assert its presence as a person through interaction with the mother.
>
> …So vital is this interaction between mother and child that my predecessor Pope Pius XII urged Catholic mothers, if at all possible, to nourish their children themselves.[6]

Mothers communicate a ministry of presence by holding and feeding their babies, by breast or bottle, but there is a beauty to God's provision through nursing that I want to share.

Through nursing, with special interaction and bonding, a mother's body sustains her baby's life, which she nurtured in her womb. The baby she protected within her during pregnancy she now protects in the safety of her arms while nursing. The baby she fed through the umbilical cord she now feeds with her milk, the perfect food, rich in her own immunities. It is always the right temperature, easily available whether at home or away.

Nursing benefits Mom as well. It releases natural pitocin, helping her uterus contract more quickly, expelling extra blood and placental material. Nursing releases "mothering" hormones that help Mom relax. Nursing also prolongs *amenses* (no periods!), giving Mom extra time to recover from pregnancy and delivery.

Women's experiences with *amenses* through nursing vary. I conceived our son Gabriel while nursing Michael, without having a complete cycle. In fact, my cycle did not return until nine months *after* weaning Gabriel. The doctor was not concerned because, unlike with use of the pill, nursing suppressed my reproductive system naturally. I had no complete cycle for four and a half years.

Nursing mediates God's grace, expressing God's care for children. "Yet you are he who took me from the womb; you kept me safe upon my mother's breasts" (Psalm 22:9). Nursing is also described as quieting a child. "But I have calmed and quieted my soul, like a child quieted at its mother's breast; like a child that is quieted is my soul" (Psalm

131:12). A nursing child is a picture of one who rests in the mother's arms.

In depicting the consolation of God's people when Jerusalem is restored, God describes the city as a nursing mother. He even describes himself as offering consolation similar to the quieting of a child at his mother's breast:

> Rejoice with Jerusalem, and be glad for her,
>   all you who love her;
> rejoice with her in joy,
>   all you who mourn over her;
> that you may suck and be satisfied
>   with her consoling breasts;
> that you may drink deeply with delight
>   from the abundance of her glory.
> …As one whom his mother comforts,
>   so I will comfort you;
>   you shall be comforted in Jerusalem.
> (Isaiah 66:10–11, 13).

The qualities that a nurturing mother possesses reflect God. Whether nursing or bottle-feeding, we want an intimate relationship with our baby. We communicate tender care as we cradle each child, establish eye contact, and speak gentle words of love.

Mom contributes to her family's well-being. Our presence contributes to the family's well-being in other ways. If you are currently working outside your home, entanglements may slow your return to the home. But what would it take to be home? What budgetary choices can be made? Can you and your spouse move in that direction, if this is your heart's desire?

As I wrote in *Chosen and Cherished,*

> A wife's contribution is real even if it is not always as tangible as a man's paycheck. She contributes...a stable presence, a ground of being for all of the members of the family. Children do not need caregivers, super-special day care centers or after-school programs. They need their mom.[7]

Not only do our children need us at home, but so do our husbands. Men experience greater peace knowing that the children are well cared for, loved, and safe. As the saying goes, "Measure wealth not by the things you have but by the things for which you would not take money."

CHAPTER EIGHT

Economics of a Stay-at-Home Mom

E very spending decision is a *spiritual* decision, because our money belongs to the Lord. "Unless the Lord builds the house, those who build it labor in vain" (Psalm 127:1a) includes financial decisions. One wife wrote, "We have decided not to build a 'dream' house because we have made a commitment to raise our future children with their mother at home. (That *is* truly the dream house of all homes.)"

Early financial decisions are important. Before you have children, live on the husband's salary, and put the wife's salary toward either debt reduction or long-term savings. Then budget to live within your means, limiting new debt. This eases the adjustment to one salary once you have a baby.

TEAMWORK FOR YOUR FINANCIAL FUTURE: BUDGET
It takes teamwork to build a financial future. Glance through Appendix C to identify which expenses apply now. (All categories do not apply every year.) Count the cost before you make major purchases.

> For which of you, desiring to build a tower, does not first sit down and count the cost, whether he has enough to complete it? Otherwise, when he has laid a foundation, and is not able to finish, all who see it begin to mock him, saying, "This man began to build, and was not able to finish." (Luke 14:28–30)

Avoid the trap of thinking you cannot afford to have a budget—you cannot afford not to budget.

Designate a monthly sum per category. Past receipts help you set limits. If you are newly married or preparing for marriage, think of budget limits as educated guesses that may need adjustment. Each month evaluate your budget and adjust totals as needed. This is a work in progress, not a decree set in stone. Be sure you agree on amounts before you begin, and be accountable to each other.

Pray before you shop—even for major expenses like weddings! For my wedding Mom clarified that the budget was $300 for a trousseau, including my gown. If I spent it all on the dress, there would be nothing extra for other clothes. It was my choice.

My sisters Kari (who was also engaged) and Kristi (still a teen) joined my mom and me to shop for a wedding gown. Before we left the driveway, Mom led in prayer.

We drove to JC Penney. The bridal department had a rack of last year's wedding dress designs. I liked several styles. Then Kari suggested, "I would be willing to wear the same dress, as long as we could alter the look." Kristi chimed in that she would love to wear the gown too, eventually.

We found a beautiful gown (a $500 gown on sale for $75) that worked for me if I wore ballet slippers and for Kari if she wore heels. Kristi's height is between ours, so the dress length could also work for her. We found the matching veil in another store (a $100 veil on sale for $25). Split three ways, the cost of our wedding gown and veil was $33.30 each. We all enjoyed wearing them, sharing a special tradition. And no one asked, "Didn't your sister wear this gown?" God provides.

When Scott and I married, money was tight. We needed to use wedding gift cash for necessities. We recorded the sum, intending to someday spend that amount on a gift with lasting value. Ten years later we took that sum from our savings and purchased some china, remembering those who had been so generous to us.

Spending with self-control. Establish a habit of spending only what you earn. (Using a cash-only system helps you control spending.) Distinguish between needs and wants. Do not compare your situation to others', desiring what they have. As Jesus cautions, "Take heed, and beware of all covetousness; for a man's life does not consist in the abundance of his possessions" (Luke 12:15).

Self-control in spending contributes long-term to the well-being of your family. "Wealth hastily gotten will dwindle, but he who gathers little by little will increase it" (Proverbs 13:11). Resist all get-rich-quick schemes, and instead invest wisely. Maintain liquidity for money needed in the near future—a rainy-day fund of six to eight months' living expenses. Then set long-term goals with money you will not need for a while. "The plans of the diligent lead surely to abundance, but every one who is hasty comes only to want" (Proverbs 21:5).

What about Christmas spending? You have options without canceling gift giving or going into debt. You can turn credit card rewards into gifts. Discover card's cash-back program allows you to double rewards for gift cards. You can take advantage of two-for-one magazine subscription deals. You can find items in original packaging at rummage sales and yard sales. You can "regift," provided you do not give the same gift back to the giver. And you can create homemade gifts that require more time than money. You can also find some great deals using the Internet.[1]

Tithing. Tithing is a budget item: We have to plan to give, as a matter of obedience. We give 10 percent of our earnings (not gifts or inheritance) to God; we live on 90 percent.

> Will man rob God? Yet you are robbing me. But you say, "How are we robbing you?" In your tithes and offerings.... Bring the full tithes into the storehouse, that there may be food in my house; and thereby put me to the test, says the LORD of hosts, if I will not open the windows of heaven for you and pour down for you an overflowing blessing. (Malachi 3:8, 10)

One friend recently challenged her husband, "Where else does God say, 'Put me to the test?'" He agreed. They increased their giving to 10 percent and watched in amazement how the Lord provided for them.

This is *not* a "health and wealth" gospel approach, as if you give to God and he will make you rich. However, we make a commitment to honor God with our finances, and he blesses our obedience.

Stewardship. Can you contribute to your family's finances apart from earning a paycheck? Yes! Regular maintenance on your appliances and equipment can extend their usefulness (see Appendix E). Keep track of your warranties so you can use them as needed. You can do a property assessment and home management analysis for needed repairs or improvements and then budget for those expenses. Over time you can enhance the beauty and value of your home.

When we needed to sell our first home, our realtor suggested we improve our home's resale value by fixing up a little-used bathroom. This small bathroom had poorly applied stucco on the walls and woodwork painted Pepto-Bismol pink. The shower leaked, so we had shut off the water. The floor was covered with well-worn carpet. (Why anyone puts carpet in bathrooms is beyond me!)

I sanded the ceiling and walls and repainted the walls and woodwork. I spent $75 total for a simple shower repair, matching curtains for the shower and window, and a remnant of linoleum. I ripped up the carpet and padding. Using newspaper, I made a pattern for the linoleum and then cut it myself, glued it down, and caulked around the walls and toilet. When the realtor returned, she upgraded our sale price. Using mostly sweat equity, I increased the value of our home by $5,000 in less than two weeks!

Do-it-yourself home improvement projects can stretch your dollars: recovering furniture; repairing garments; purchasing furniture, fabric, and wallpaper at yard sales; and gardening vegetables, flowers, and herbs. I have saved thousands of dollars by hanging my own wallpaper and sewing window treatments. And I experienced increased satisfaction due to the savings and the finished product.

Moms can assist each other: One watches the children while the other paints or wallpapers. Families can swap work in carpentry or plumbing. Just because your father's do-it-yourself move was to dial an expert does not mean that you cannot learn these skills yourself. And you set a great example for your children.

Rather than compare your home to others', choose contentment. "Keep your life free from love of money, and be content with what you have" (Hebrews 13:5a).

AVOID DEBT

Debt mortgages the future, limiting options. Since men and women cannot enter religious life with debt, some vocations are delayed years due to paying off loans. Many people assume that it is OK to enter marriage with debt. However, money issues rank high as a reason for divorce.

Before you acquire (more) debt, ask some critical questions. Is the return greater than the cost? Education debt may enable you to provide a better living for your family; consumptive debt for furniture or appliances may limit your future choices. How will you repay the loan? Do both you and your spouse have peace of mind about assuming this debt after you have prayed about it?

Credit cards make it possible to live beyond our means but at a high cost. People average a third more spending when they can use a card rather than cash. Do you pay your credit card bill in full every month? If so, you avoid extra charges. If, however, you feel buried by credit card debt or barely able to pay monthly minimums, cancel all cards (except one for emergencies), and switch to cash only. Then focus on one card at a time, starting with either the card on which you owe the least or the one on which you pay the highest interest, and each month pay off as much debt as possible.

Is there someone for whom you have great respect in financial matters? Seek his or her advice, for "where there is no guidance, a people falls; but in an abundance of counselors there is safety" (Proverbs 11:14). Years ago we were challenged about car debt by financial advisor Ron Blue. He taught that the cheapest car to have is one you own until repairs cost more than its value. Our car may not look as nice as the neighbor's or hold as many people, but it is ours to use while we save toward our next car.

We had saved $1,500 toward our next car when the expenses for our daughter's birth wiped out our savings. At the same time a mechanic said our car would not last another winter. We prayed and decided we would do what we could to keep our car running. If it died, we would go into debt for a car.

That car made it through *two* more winters. When it was on its last leg, my mother-in-law spotted a van for sale. We had $3,000 in savings. After a test-drive we bought it for $2,750. We only had $250 left, but we owned the car debt-free.

Do you barely pay off one car before you need a new one? It is cheaper—and there is greater freedom—if you pay in full for a car instead of taking out a loan. Then save toward the next car, rather than continually acquiring cars with debt. The difference in cost may not be that great, but it is the difference between debt and freedom. As Proverbs warns, "The borrower is the slave of the lender" (Proverbs 22:7b).

What about buying a home? You do not need to purchase a home like the one your parents currently own or better. It is possible to purchase one of lesser quality, fix it up, and pay down principal as much as you can, so that you can build equity toward purchasing the home of your dreams. You also do not need to purchase a home before you have a child: Children can be raised in an apartment. If you want Mom to be home with the children, do not purchase a home that makes that impossible. Think before you purchase.

Most likely you cannot purchase a home without a mortgage. Having paid off debt improves your credit rating; having existing debt may prohibit a mortgage. Take time to call local banks to compare kinds of mortgages available, rates for fifteen-, twenty-, and thirty-year mortgages, and whether or not there are fees if you pay off the loan early. Ask the bank for an amortization schedule, so that you know each month how much of your payment goes toward interest and how much toward principal.[2]

Most of your initial mortgage payments go toward interest. Any additional money you can pay toward principal—including gifts from parents or grandparents—will eliminate months or possibly years of your mortgage. The goal is to be completely debt-free as soon as possible.

CONTENTMENT OR CONTENTIOUSNESS

The Proverbs 31 woman chooses contentment. She maintains calm self-possession, placing her trust in the Lord. In contrast to a fool who ignores wisdom and is destroyed, she "who listens to me will dwell secure and will be at ease, without dread of evil" (Proverbs 1:33).

The choice she makes—and we have to make—is, will I be content or become contentious? Proverbs addresses this: "It is better to live in a corner of the housetop than in a house shared with a contentious woman…. It is better to live in a desert land than with a contentious and fretful woman" (Proverbs 21:9, 19). Saint Paul says, "Not that I complain of want; for I have learned, in whatever state I am, to be content. I know how to be abased, and I know how to abound;

in any and all circumstances I have learned the secret of facing plenty and hunger, abundance and want" (Philippians 4:11–12). For the good of our marriage and family life, we need to choose contentment.

How can the Proverbs 31 woman laugh at the time to come? Is she a silly woman who does not take future concerns seriously? Hardly! She does not need to know the future in order *not* to fear it. She laughs at the time to come because *she knows the One who knows the future.* Though circumstances may change, God does not: "For I the LORD do not change" (Malachi 3:6a). We also can face the future because we trust the Lord.

CHAPTER NINE

Mary, Model for Mothers

As a Protestant, I believed that Mary was the virgin mother of Jesus, but she had no place in my life. She was a disciple, but so were many others. I do not recall a sermon on Mary's *fiat*, her loving care for Jesus as his mother, or her devotion to him all the way to the cross. Now I feel how tragic it is that Mary is ignored by so many who love her son, especially when imitation of Christ is at the heart of Christian practice.

Mary is our spiritual mother and model disciple. How did she face an uncertain future? She gave consent to the will of God in a variety of ways.

Consent to the unknown (see Luke 1:26–38). Though Mary knows it will bring a mix of joy and suffering, she surrenders to God's will that she become the mother of the Messiah. Through her consent she receives the gift of motherhood; he does not merely take up residence within her. She not only provides her womb, in which Jesus grows, but she is the source of Jesus' flesh and blood.

She is the only mother whose *son created her*. Through Mary Jesus becomes the God-man, our Savior, through whom we receive life. Mary's humble response to the angel's announcement is neither a prideful "You picked the right woman!" nor a false humility, "I could never raise the Son of God." She simply states her willingness to be available to do whatever God has called her to do.

Like Mary, will we consent to bear new life or face new challenges without knowing the parameters of how much will be required of us? Will we be available?

Consent to serve (see Luke 1:39–56.) Though Mary is newly pregnant, she goes immediately more than seventy miles to serve her cousin, Elizabeth, who is already six months pregnant. Elizabeth, filled with the Holy Spirit, declares to all that Mary is uniquely blessed as the mother of her Lord. Mary responds with her Magnificat, acknowledging God's tremendous work within her as he fulfills his promises to bring salvation. Mary stays with Elizabeth for three months, serving her. Then Mary travels home to complete her pregnancy.

Mary chooses to serve without asking to be served. She reminds us of Jesus' words during his ministry: "For the Son of man also came not to be served but to serve, and to give his life as a ransom for many" (Mark 10:45).

Will we, like Mary, consent to serve even when we do not feel like it?

Consent to follow her husband (see Matthew 2:13–15). Mary willingly travels with Joseph to Bethlehem to register their family in obedience to the Roman authorities. She trusts Joseph to care for her and the baby, far away from their families, who could have assisted them at delivery. Then she births Jesus in a cave outside of Bethlehem.

When Joseph tells her that an angel has warned them to flee, Mary does not second-guess him, claiming that usually angels tell her what to do. She packs up their belongings and follows Joseph into a foreign land, doing what she can to preserve Jesus' life. Mary follows the promptings of her heart and the word of the Lord through her husband.

Will we, like Mary, follow our husband's lead, especially when it comes to the well-being of our children?

Consent to a hidden life (see Matthew 2:19–23; Luke 2:19, 21–35, 39–52). Though Mary knows the prophecy Simeon gave her—that a sword will pierce her heart—she embraces motherhood, the joys and the sorrows. She exemplifies for us that the call to be open to life is a call to lay down our lives.

Mary loves Jesus. She nurses him and cares for him. With Joseph she takes him to the temple to be circumcised. She celebrates the Jewish feast days with him, like Passover in Jerusalem. She raises Jesus, knowing she does not fully understand him. She ponders God's work in her life (see Luke 2:19). For thirty (hidden) years Mary lives with Jesus. Mary is "the incomparable model of how life should be welcomed and cared for."[1]

Scott and I traveled with our infant son Jeremiah for a speaking engagement. After I settled him for the night, I worked on my talk. Very late, just as I was creeping into bed, I heard Jeremiah's peep. I leapt out of bed to keep Scott from waking and nursed Jeremiah.

Four times I thought he was asleep in the crib, only to crawl between the covers and hear him begin to peep again! I was tense; I am sure the baby sensed it.

The last time I jumped up, angry. I had a talk to give in just a few hours! Immediately I knew my attitude was wrong. This was not the baby's fault. I felt the Lord say to me, pick him up as you would pick *me* up!

Gratitude flooded my heart: oh, to pick up Jesus! Tenderly I picked Jeremiah up, placing him on my shoulder. In my heart I said, it's OK, little one, if you don't even sleep tonight. It's God's problem if I am not coherent tomorrow.

I was at peace, and of course, Jeremiah immediately fell into a deep sleep. I thanked God for the reminder of how I should approach my children. After I laid him down, the four hours' rest I got was ample to deliver my talk. How kind of God to help me see my child through Mary's eyes.

Undoubtedly Mary treasured time with her son. But did she, like us, find the time went too quickly, and he was no longer a baby, a toddler, a teen? Do we take time to ponder God's great work in our lives and our children's lives?

Consent to love at a distance (see Luke 11:27–28). Mary does not accompany Jesus everywhere he ministers, though others do. She supports him from a distance and binds her heart to his through prayer.

While Jesus is teaching a crowd, one woman proclaims a blessing on his mother: "Blessed is the womb that bore you, and the breasts that you sucked!" (Luke 11:27b). Jesus refocuses the crowd's attention. He does not downgrade the debt he owes Mary as his mother. Instead he highlights the impetus for her actions that others, like us, can imitate. "Blessed rather are those who hear the word of God and keep it!" (Luke 11:28). Mary's obedient response to God's Word, no matter the cost, is blessed. She is obedient in great and small things; therein lies her greatness.

Do we, like Mary, allow an adult child to assert his or her independence, all the while communicating our love, respect, and support? Do we love from a distance? Do we bind our hearts to theirs in prayer?

Consent to suffer: Our Lady of Sorrows (see John 19:25–27). Our Lord needed his heavenly Father *and* his earthly mother, all the way to the cross. Accompanying Christ to Calvary,

Mary consented to his sacrificial self-offering with her own self-offering.

When Jeremiah was two, we discovered we were pregnant. We shared the wonderful news with the children and went to Mass in celebration. Three days later I began to miscarry. We shared the sad news with the children just before we went to Mass. My heart was heavy as I grieved for this child, our third miscarriage. The responsorial psalm referred to a "sacrifice of praise." I prayed, "I *will* praise you, Lord, as a sheer act of my will; but I will always be sad that I never held these three little ones."

Until this time Mary's title "Our Lady of Sorrows" bothered me. She was Jesus' mother—surely there was no need to focus on the negative with such a sad title. At that moment the Lord spoke to my heart: "And how could my mother *not* be Our Lady of Sorrows, since she held in her arms the lifeless body she gave me?" All of a sudden I understood her title. My life, like Mary's, has had moments of agony that do not detract from the unspeakable joys I have had as well.

Will we, like Mary, offer our sufferings and losses, choosing to trust the Lord for what we do not understand?

Consent to continue to serve even when her child is gone. Mary's work is not done once Jesus is gone. From the cross, in the midst of his anguish, Jesus gives his mother to the Beloved Disciple, which includes giving her to us as beloved disciples as well. Mary receives him—and us—as her child (see John 19:26–27). Mary lingers with the disciples in the Upper Room at Pentecost. She leaves her homeland and travels to Ephesus, Turkey, with Saint John, and she is probably the source for Saint Luke's infancy narratives. She reminds widows, widowers, empty nesters, and retirees there is more work to do!

Will we, like Mary, continue to serve the Lord as we get older, welcoming opportunities to care for others in Jesus' name?

A PENNY FOR YOUR THOUGHTS (AND PRAYERS)

Raised Protestant, I did not find it easy to feel an emotional connection to Mary. I grew up thinking about Jesus most of the time, which is wonderful. But I had no idea how to acknowledge Mary as a part of my life until a college student shared an idea with me. Whenever her mother found a penny, she gave it to her daughter and said, "Never forget, your mother loves you."

I adapted this simple but beautiful idea. Whenever I find a penny, I thank God for Mary's love for me. Next I thank Mary directly for her love and prayers for me. Then I give the penny to one of my children, saying, "Never forget, Mommy loves you, Mimi and Grandma love you, and Mother Mary loves you."

I have found pennies in unusual places—on a car after I crashed, on a desk in a freshly cleaned hotel room, on a pew, and under ice in a parking lot. I even found an Italian penny on a Rome sidewalk. When I used to walk with my dear friends Marianne and Deb in our neighborhood, we routinely found one or two pennies, reminding each other of Mary's love for us. The day we had a seven-penny walk we could hardly contain our joy! I am so grateful for Mary's care for me.

Mary accompanies us on our journey as we carry our cross.

She prays for us, joining us before the throne of her son. As a mother swaddles a child to keep him from scratching his face, so Mary wraps us in her mantle to keep us from harming ourselves or others. Mary faced the future with faith, and we should imitate her.

By God's grace—with the Proverbs 31 woman and the Blessed Virgin Mary, our mother—we can laugh at the time to come.

PART FOUR

Her Husband

Is Known

in the Gates

CHAPTER TEN

The Perfect Parent

The husband of the Proverbs 31 woman enjoys a good reputation. "Her husband is known in the gates, when he sits among the elders of the land" (verse 23). His reputation is established through his wife's management of the home and the obedience of his children, fitting the criteria Saint Paul gives for bishops of the early Church (before mandatory celibacy). "He must manage his own household well, keeping his children submissive and respectful in every way; for if a man does not know how to manage his own household, how can he care for God's Church?" (1 Timothy 3:4–5).

The wife is key to the husband's leadership in the home. "A good wife is the crown of her husband, but she who brings shame is like rottenness in his bones" (Proverbs 12:4). What long-term consequences do a wife's actions and words have for her husband? Does she tear down his reputation or build it up?

The Proverbs 31 woman contributes to the well-being of her community, which draws on her husband's respected leadership. He is "known in the gates," the place where legal disputes are resolved (see Ruth 4:11). He "sits among the elders," the highly respected men of the town who are considered wise in their judgments. He is not a young man: His family has developed, and his children are mature.

An "expert" began giving a talk on parenting when he was newly married with no children. His talk was entitled "Six

Keys to Successful Parenting." After his firstborn arrived, he changed the title to "Tried and True Principles for Parenting." Another child and a couple of years later, he advertised "Good Guidelines for Good Parents." Last I heard, his parenting talk was simply called "Helpful Hints for Fellow Strugglers!"

Please know that what I share as a parent, I share as a fellow struggler. Like you, I long to "do it right." I am also looking for resources, tips, plans, strategies, and above all, wisdom. Hopefully what I share in these pages will be a measure of what I have learned from others.

GOD THE FATHER

What does it take to be the perfect parent? Let's look at God the Father. He chose to create us before the world began (see Ephesians 1:4). He delights in us and loves us (Hebrews 12:6). He is present to us. (*Emmanuel* literally means "God with us" [Matthew 1:23b].)

He governs us with wisdom. "Hear, my son, and accept my words, that the years of your life may be many. I have taught you the way of wisdom; I have led you in the paths of uprightness" (Proverbs 4:10–11). Wisdom is part of our inheritance (see Sirach 4:16).

God the Father lavishes grace on his children, giving us good gifts (see Matthew 7:9–11). He is slow to anger and kind. His forbearance is meant to lead us to repentance. "But you are a God ready to forgive, gracious and merciful, slow to anger and abounding in mercy, and did not forsake them" (Nehemiah 9:17b).

God the Father has given us free will. He expects us to obey—even requires obedience—but he does not force us to obey. He reproves us and wants us to respond with humility (see Proverbs 3:11–12). He leads us toward habits of obedience. "Therefore you correct little by little those who trespass, and remind and warn them of the things wherein they sin, that they may be freed from wickedness and put their trust in you, O LORD" (Wisdom 12:2). He wants us to trust him. "But those who have not heeded the warning of light rebukes will experience the deserved judgment of God" (Wisdom 12:26). There are consequences to our disobedience, even to future generations (see Exodus 20:5–6).

Discipline, including punishment, is an essential part of parenting. Our heavenly Father "disciplines us for our good, that we may share his holiness" (Hebrews 12:10). Though we might want to punish a neighbor child, we would not; he is not our child. God's discipline proves we really are his children.

Even God, the perfect parent, has rebellious kids, "Hear, O heavens, and give ear, O earth; for the LORD has spoken: 'Sons have I reared and brought up, but they have rebelled against me'" (Isaiah 1:2). How does God respond? He continues to love them through discipline that at times is painful. The pain, however, is not retribution. It has a purpose: "later it yields the peaceful fruit of righteousness to those who have been trained by it" (Hebrews 12:11b). God the Father's goal is to restore our relationship to him.

The Privilege of Parenting

Parenting is a privilege. "[P]arenting is a call to form *persons*. We're called to bring God to our children's spirits, truth to their minds, health to their bodies, skill to their hands, beauty and creativity to their hearts, and in all this, virtue to their wills and sanctity to their souls."[1]

God has placed these particular children in our care. "For the Lord honored the father above the children, and he confirmed the right of the mother over her sons" (Sirach 3:2). We are called to meet our children's primary needs: unconditional love, a sense of belonging, and consistent discipline. We nurture them emotionally, intellectually, physically, and spiritually. We help them develop virtues, establish values, set goals, and shape their convictions within the context of our family.

One of our greatest challenges as parents is maintaining perspective. Each day we adjust our vision as we would bring a camera lens into focus. Why am I doing what I am doing? For love of Jesus, my spouse, and my children.

We maintain perspective by prayer and a sense of humor. We have been called to juggle bowling balls—with grace! I am reminded of the time that a visiting priest was hearing my confession in the living room. Every family member, including my husband, stopped by and interrupted with something. The priest had barely pronounced absolution and said, "Go in peace," when the front door slammed shut and a child yelled at the top of his lungs, "MOM!"

I felt as if I were a jockey at the start of a race. I guess we ride better if we sit loose in the saddle, and that is what a sense of humor enables us to do.

Parents With S.O.F.T. Hearts

We parent with firm convictions and S.O.F.T. hearts. Let me explain.

Sacrificial love. Like God, we embrace the sacrifices involved in loving our children unconditionally. Love for our spouse, reflected in each child, further inspires sacrifices.

Obedient heart. We obey the Lord by training our children. To be an effective authority, we have to be under authority. Our children learn from our example. We train them to obey us so that they have hearts ready to obey the Lord.

Forgiving heart. God, who is rich in mercy, calls us to govern our children with grace. We parent with "tenderness, forgiveness, respect, fidelity, and disinterested service" (*CCC*, 2223). If there is a pattern of poor behavior, we address it as a habit without going through a litany of past offenses.

Thankful heart. We thank God daily for each child, knowing he or she is a special blessing to us and to our family. We recognize his or her unique gifts and abilities and pray for the wisdom to know how to help each one develop to his or her full potential.

Our overall goal is to have happy, healthy, and holy children who obey us and obey God. As parents we have limitations. Unlike God, we are not omniscient, omnipresent, nor omnipotent; we are not expected to be. God asks what is possible, by his grace. We, in turn, entrust each child to God to make up for all that we lack. We pray for wisdom, which he will give to us: "If any of you lacks wisdom, let him ask God, who gives to all men generously and without reproaching, and it will be given him" (James 1:5). We are imperfect parents parenting imperfect children imperfectly! This is God's plan.

IMITATE GOD'S WAY OF PARENTING

We begin with our delight in each child. We love our children before they have done anything to merit that love. Our children love us because we first loved them, just as God the Father first loved us.

To parent effectively, we become students of each child. We learn their likes and dislikes. It takes time, but we observe each unfolding personality and emerging temperament.

Regarding personality, is your child an introvert or an extrovert?[2] Does he process information in an intuitive or sensory way? Does he weigh his words before speaking or blurt out his thoughts? Is he a go-with-the-flow guy or more of an organized planner?

In terms of temperament, is he more of a sanguine, melancholic, choleric, or phlegmatic person—or a combination?[3] What strengths and weaknesses are natural to his temperament? How can you guide him to understand certain natural tendencies for virtues and vices?

What is the primary way each child expresses love? In *The Five Love Languages of Children*, Dr. Gary Chapman explains five ways in which love is interpreted and expressed, similar to languages.[4]

I understood this analogy better after I attended a general audience at the Vatican. It was awe-inspiring: thousands of people responding to Pope John Paul II as he greeted them in their native tongue. When Pope John Paul II greeted a Japanese group in their language, they immediately stood and listened in rapt attention. When he finished, they burst into applause. It was moving to witness, but it paled in comparison for me once he began to speak in English. He had my full attention: I was hanging on every word.

Love languages likewise draw our attention when they correspond to our own. Here is a brief description:

Words of affirmation include genuine compliments, especially in front of other people, as well as notes of praise.

Quality time is time together, sharing heart to heart.

Gift giving refers to gifts or treats that communicate you thought of someone when you were not together.

Acts of service consist of noticing others' needs and meeting them without being asked.

Physical touch and closeness involves physical contact, like wrestling and back rubs, or physical affection.

Dr. Chapman asserts that one love language is more significant than the others to each child. If we can identify that language, we can communicate love to that child more effectively. Some have the same love language for both giving and receiving; others differ as they give or receive. If the love languages of your children seem tricky to identify, consider their complaints: that may indicate their primary language. No matter what the distinct love language of a child, we should speak all of the languages to each child.

Track personal information for each child on three-by-five cards. One card lists favorite foods and drinks. Another notes current clothing sizes and preferences of color and style. One card inventories gifts already purchased, while another records gift suggestions. One card documents financial information (bank account and Social Security numbers). Another contains updated health information, such as the latest medical, dental, and eye exams, current prescriptions for glasses and contacts, and immunization schedules. An additional card details contact information for teachers and schools, coaches and tutors.

THE VIRTUE OF OBEDIENCE

We do not train a child the way we train a dog. Our dog may heed a command, but it does not have the virtue of obedience. Instead we approach each child with the respect and dignity of a person who bears the image of God. We consider our child's well-being in this life and the next, as we help him or her develop the virtue of obedience.

We build on our love for and knowledge of our child with discipline. Discipline does not equal punishment. The root of the word *discipline* is *disciple*. We *disciple* our child through our example and instruction. (Chapters twelve and thirteen cover teaching our child the faith in detail.) We teach right behavior and correct wrong behavior with lots of love, prayer, and common sense.

We clarify the behavior we expect. "Train up a child in the way he should go, and when he is old he will not depart from it" (Proverbs 22:6). Either train a child in right living now, and even when he is old he will still follow your instruction, or allow a child to go the way he wants, without direction, and even when he is old he will not change his ways.

It is as if we are setting rails on which a train can run, so that the train will reach its destination. No matter how powerful the train, it will be unable to proceed without rails on which to run. The goal is not freedom without limits, but freedom within limits.

Children do not know their needs; we do. Whether or not they want to, they have to bathe, eat, change, and go to bed per our directions. They are not totally depraved—that is an abstraction. Nor are they pure innocents without self-centeredness: Their ongoing struggle with sin, concupiscence, is real.

Our attitude needs to be one of calm, firm confidence. We are gently guiding a soul, not corralling a wild horse, though occasionally we see a wilder side.

One Ash Wednesday I prepared Jeremiah, then two, for receiving ashes. After giving me mine, the priest refused to touch Jeremiah's forehead, saying, "No, children do not sin." My normally compliant child screamed, "I want my ashes! Give me my ashes!" all the way back to the pew. I hoped the priest heard him disprove his theory.

Every interaction we have with our child *is* an act of formation. Will we form him to be patient or impatient? Kind or unkind? Generous or stingy? Will we persist in this task, year after year, knowing that it will produce good fruit eventually? "Discipline your son while there is hope; do not set your heart on his destruction" (Proverbs 19:18). If we grow weary of guiding our child, we consign him to destruction; if we endure through the challenges, we can expect maturity.

The bad news: It is harder to impose boundaries after a child has been poorly disciplined. The good news: It is never too late to work on discipline techniques and recommit to follow through. I saw an analogy for this when we planted tomatoes.

Tomato cages create supports that help plants thrive, limit access to bugs, and make weeding and harvesting easier. Without supports the plants grow, but they do not bear much fruit. However, it is never too late to add supports. Some damage will occur fitting the sprawling limbs inside the boundaries of the wire cages, but better fruit will come. Parents who discipline their children provide the support children need to thrive, but the later they start, the harder it is.

What are important lifelong goals we have for children? Proverbs 1—6 record many: understand and know God; enjoy long life, abundant welfare, and spiritual life; find favor with God and man; gain wisdom to live moral lives. All of these marvelous goals are linked to the virtue of obedience (see Proverbs 1:8; 2:1–5; 3:21–22; 4:1–2; 5:1–2, 7; 6:20–24).

We guide our children's growth in virtue by small degrees. We can miss it if we do not pay attention.

Once a week I record a specific prayer for character development for each child. The next week I thank God for answers to that prayer, and I note new challenges. Sometimes I document strengths and weaknesses I see emerging as well. I refer to these as "shoehorn" prayers—a shoehorn slips into a tight space and eases the transition of the foot into the shoe for a good fit. I offer prayers for the tight spaces in the lives of my loved ones, to ease their transitions by grace. Praying specifically and noting answers to prayer brings great encouragement to me, especially as I reread the journals. God is at work in all of us.

MODELS OF PARENTING

Models of parenting vary based on the demands of discipline and the demonstration of love. We will briefly look at the following models: authoritarian, permissive, neglectful, and authoritative.

The authoritarian parent does not express much warmth or encouragement. He or she emphasizes discipline with a high degree of control. This parent maintains high control as the child matures. At first a child complies. Eventually the child expresses anger either in a passive-aggressive mode—the only safe way to cause trouble—or in outright rebellion. This child tends to have low self-esteem.

The permissive parent expresses much love but little discipline. This parent hesitates to restrict the child; the child is in control. Though the child feels loved, he or she does not sense that the parent cares enough to guide him. "He who spoils his son will bind up his wounds, and his feelings will be troubled at every cry.... A son unrestrained turns out to be willful" (Sirach 30:7, 8b). When the child gets older, the parent may try to tighten the rules. Usually the result is great frustration: The rules have changed, and the child resists restrictions. This child is vulnerable to peer pressure.

The neglectful parent offers little love or discipline. The child longs for both and feels anger from broken promises and neglect. "The rod and reproof give wisdom, but a child left to himself brings shame to his mother" (Proverbs 29:15). This child's low self-esteem makes him vulnerable to identifying with a counterculture, at risk to himself and others.

The authoritative parent leads with lots of love and affection *and* lots of discipline. The parent exercises authority with rules that vary depending on the child's age and maturity. The child learns to respond well to authority and to hold his own with peers. Overall this child understands parental boundaries and values the relationship between greater freedoms and greater responsibilities. This leads to a positive self-image for the child.

PARENTS IN TRANSITION

A sports analogy helps us visualize the transition from parental control to a child's self-control.

First, a parent is a kind of *trainer*. Day in, day out, the parent requires obedience. He teaches the rules of the game of life. He clarifies foul lines and the penalties when fouls are committed. He requires the child to follow his lead.

Second, the parent's role changes to a *player-coach*. He invites the child to make some decisions in the game of life. The player-coach still calls the plays, but the child has greater freedom to participate in decisions.

Third, the parent steps off the field and *coaches* from the sidelines. He still calls play options, and he may occasionally halt play. But he allows the child to determine more decisions. He offers guidance and suggestions more often than commands.

Finally, the parent is like the *sports announcer*. He announces plays the child makes. He offers analysis and praise when appropriate. The parent helps the child discern the wisdom of certain decisions. He emphasizes the good, even in failures, and offers advice when asked. At all times the child is aware that the parent believes in him and is doing what he can to help him toward independence.

One challenge some of us face is parenting at different stages of life across a spread of ages. We may be trainer to one while already sports announcer to another. We can trip up easily if we are not careful to switch discipline strategies from toddler to teen.

A disciplined child brings great joy to his mother and father. "The father of the righteous will greatly rejoice; he who begets a wise son will be glad in him. Let your father and mother be glad, let her who bore you rejoice" (Proverbs 23:24–25).

THE NECESSITY OF FATHERS

Fathers can be an indispensable reflection of God the Father to their children.

My husband worked for a summer in the inner city of Pittsburgh with four former Black Panthers who had become Christians. The first day he referred to God the Father. One of the men corrected him. He was *not* to refer to God as Father, since almost all of the teens had had difficult experiences with their fathers. The dads were either absent or drunk and abusive, hurting them and their mothers.

Scott urged the leaders to take a different approach. Since the fathers had failed, the only hope for a new generation of young men was to help them know God as Father. Their heavenly Father could be trusted to keep his promises; he was faithful in his loving care. The leaders agreed.

By God's grace fathers can imitate God the Father. They can love their children better because they receive the Father's love personally. They can provide safety because they have found safety in the Lord. "The name of the LORD is a strong tower; the righteous man runs into it and is safe" (Proverbs 18:10).

Dads are essential in the development of their children: Children do not just need a parent; they need both mother *and* father. Dads are critical to the purity of their daughters. They communicate the dignity and worth of each young woman through their unconditional love. Dads are also important in the maturity of their sons. They provide healthy outlets for their energy in work and play, reinforce their desires to protect and defend those weaker than themselves, and help them control their emerging strength.

Fathers provide future orientation for the family. They help their children see their potential. They motivate them to work hard toward goals. They focus on character building more than comfort, spurring their children toward larger life goals.

THE STRENGTH OF A FATHER

Fathers need to know their own strength and its limits. "Rely not on your own strength in following the desires of your heart" (Sirach 5:2, *NAB*). Instead fathers provide a refuge for their children *when* they rely on the strength of God their Father. "Every word of God proves true; he is a shield to those who take refuge in him" (Proverbs 30:5). If a dad guides his family with wisdom, "he will place his children under her [wisdom's] shelter" (Sirach 14:26a).

Some dads are larger and louder than they realize. "Do not be like a lion in your home" (Sirach 4:30a). What will they do with their strength? They can use it to protect loved ones or to make them feel attacked.

When a father shares his strength with his family, he gives them a sense of shelter. "Each will be like a hiding place from the wind, a covert from the tempest, like streams of water in a dry place, like the shade of a great rock in a weary land" (Isaiah 32:2). A father's strength is a gift, especially when family members feel his strength *for* them.

Wives must support their husbands as these men learn to be fathers. Hopefully wives will appreciate their husband's gift of strength, and if it is misused, they will communicate privately about it. At all times wives should encourage an attitude of love and respect from the children toward their dad (see Sirach 3:3–9).

THE DANGER OF DISCIPLINING WITH ANGER

Warning: There is a danger of D.U.I., Discipline Under the Influence (of anger). This can be a problem for fathers or mothers.

"A man without self-control is like a city broken into and left without walls" (Proverbs 25:28). When a father disciplines in anger, he is in danger of losing self-control and harming or hurting a child, physically or verbally. The child can feel the lack of safety and protection, like a city whose protective walls have crumbled. "A man of quick temper acts foolishly, but a man of discretion is patient" (Proverbs 14:17).

It is possible to be angry without sin. "Be angry but do not sin; do not let the sun go down on your anger, and give no opportunity to the devil" (Ephesians 4:26–27). However, often anger is expressed in a way that brings more harm than good. "A fool gives full vent to his anger, but a wise man quietly holds it back" (Proverbs 29:11). Saint Paul specifically addresses fathers in his letter to the believers at Colossae: "Children, obey your parents in everything, for this pleases the Lord. Fathers, do not provoke your children, lest they become discouraged" (Colossians 3:20–21).

Mothers can get angry too. One morning I did what I do not recommend: I tried to juggle housework, laundry, and homeschooling. I set up the boys with their schoolwork and left to complete a task. Gabriel, age four, was dawdling with a simple assignment. Instead of helping him, I became impatient. I took him by the hand and marched him to the next room. "You just sit here and think about it!"

Gabriel looked up at me with tears in his eyes. "I don't want to go to heaven!"

I could not believe my ears. "Why are you dragging heaven into this?"

His reply cut me to the quick. "'Cuz I don't want to live with you forever."

Immediately I saw what I had done. "Oh, Gabe, I wouldn't want to live with me forever either." I dropped to my knees, "Honey, please forgive Mommy for being harsh with you." He forgave me quickly, and with a hug we were back on track.

In a weak response to a child's disobedience, mothers tend to plead or whine, and men tend to fume and bellow. Neither response expresses parental maturity. Instead we must regain our composure before we respond to our child, for "a soft answer turns away wrath, but a harsh word stirs up anger" (Proverbs 15:1). We want to offer a peaceful response that quells a quarrel instead of expressing "anger and its fruits: irritability, fault-finding, criticism, peevishness, uncharitableness, spread discord and discontent."[5]

An older woman observed a young mother pushing a grocery cart with her young child seated. More than once they passed, and each time the older woman heard the mother say, "Barbara, be patient…. You can do this…. Barbara, we're almost done."

When the older woman found herself behind this mom at the checkout, she leaned forward and said, "Ma'am, you are so patient with Barbara."

To which the young mother responded, "*I'm* Barbara!" Her encouraging words for patience and self-control were directed at herself. Her daughter was the secondary beneficiary of her calm demeanor.

We must guard our words and attitudes in expressing anger. Saint James cautions, "Know this, my beloved brethren. Let every man be quick to hear, slow to speak, slow to anger, for the anger of man does not work the righteousness of God" (James 1:19–20).

One day I took my three little ones to Mass. I was convicted during Mass that I had been harsh with them that morning, especially trying to get to Mass! This is the only time that I have chosen to receive the Eucharist in my hand. I wanted to remember that the hand that had touched Jesus should only touch my children as Jesus would.

Fr. James McElhone wrote,

> Even temper, the holding of anger in check, is the bringing of self-love into subjection.... Even temper is attractive, helps the community spirit, keeps down all that tends to anger, for it seeks under varying circumstances to be pleasant, amiable, agreeable, mild, patient.... [I]t is the getting along with others through a constant and insistent practice of charity.[6]

For information about conflict resolution and anger management, see chapter ten of my book *Chosen and Cherished: Biblical Wisdom for Your Marriage*. It applies to parenting as well as marriage. A chart called "The Anger Ladder" helps identify steps to growth in self-control. This is especially important when we want to correct misbehavior without anger: It is an opportunity for us to model the virtue of obedience for our children.

CHAPTER ELEVEN

Bringing Up Children With Discipline and Instruction

D iscipline is an expression of committed parental love. In Ephesians 6:4 Saint Paul uses two Greek words to describe the task of parenting: "bring them up in the discipline [*piduw*] and instruction [*nouthetew*] of the Lord." *Piduw* also means "nurture, admonish, correct, chastise, and reprove." Parents provide this kind of guidance primarily to younger children. *Nouthetew* refers to instruction appropriate for older children and adults. Parents never complete this lifelong task.

The goal of discipline is this: Teach a child to obey his parents so that he will yield his heart to God his Father. Discipline involves right actions and attitudes; more importantly, it develops a child's virtues and restrains vices. Discipline is not about parents controlling children but about their guiding children toward self-control.

It is important to set boundaries within which a child can thrive. What does a boundary accomplish?

A fenced-in yard protects a child. It temporarily restricts freedom until a child is mature enough to expand the boundaries. Family rules and God's laws provide boundaries within which a child can thrive until the appropriate time for greater independence.

Five Keys to Setting Boundaries With Young Children

When your baby begins exploring your home by crawling and then walking, you realize you need boundaries or rules to guide your child. Have you set C.L.E.A.R. boundaries for your child's safety and well-being?

Committed to consistency. Remember the rules and enforce them. Require first-time obedience. Delayed obedience is disobedience. Does your child obey only after you convince him that he must? You want your child to understand why the rules exist; however, you do not owe him an explanation before he obeys. (I accept "OK, why?" as long as the child sincerely accepts the directive and asks "Why?" for clarification rather than a delay tactic.)

Chore charts help with consistency. If you post duty lists, your child knows his jobs for the week, and you know who is responsible for what. If a chore chart includes steps to complete a task, your child knows your expectations, and you will know what job to expect. Arguments and emotional outbursts are kept to a minimum.

Consistency means you apply the same rules to each child—no favorites. Resist the extremes of hypercontrol of your firstborn and lack of control over your youngest. Consistency requires long-term thinking and planning. "And let us not grow weary in well-doing, for in due season we shall reap, if we do not lose heart" (Galatians 6:9).

Limits. Establish reasonable, age-appropriate limits to your child's freedom. To be sure that he understands the limits, ask him to repeat the rules. Give choices where possible. For instance, he can serve his own food, but what he takes he must eat. (Encourage small portions at first with the possibility of seconds if he is still hungry.) For another example, review time limits with your child for watching TV or using the computer. Then be sure he can gauge the time with a clock, a timer, or a watch.

Enforceable consequences. Explain consequences for disobedience. Does your child understand? Ask him to repeat what the consequences are. If he disobeys, follow through—no idle threats. Your response should be timely without major delays. If your child is defiant, you need to win the showdown—for his good.

Adjust. Anticipate adjustments without waiting until your child complains. Adjust rules based on age (bedtimes or Internet time to accommodate school assignments) or circumstances (like visits to grandparents). Greater maturity leads to more opportunities, while less maturity decreases opportunities.

Responsibilities are linked to privileges. Let your child know how much you want him to succeed. You want him to mature into greater privileges and greater freedoms. After he bikes in the neighborhood, does he put his bike away? When he goes to a friend's home, does he call to signal his safe arrival? Irresponsibility equals a loss of privileges; responsibility equals greater privileges.

FAMILY RULES

How can you develop family rules? Elisabeth Elliot gives this advice: "Praying together for wisdom and standing together on all matters of discipline should be a rule for parents."[1] As husband and wife, working together, you differentiate between absolutes to obey (law) and ideas from friends or family (wisdom) that may or may not apply in your family. Establish the rules and review them regularly.

Family rules fall under various categories: bedtimes (school nights, weekends, summertime), schedules (including family meals and other commitments), pop culture (what is acceptable in music and movies), table manners, homework or homeschooling (when and where it should be done), dress code (modesty, cleanliness), computer use (schoolwork, personal use), chores (how many, how often), friends (sleepovers, parties), TV watching (how much, when). Your rules may be in flux, but once established, do your best to enforce them.

Seven Strategies for Correcting Misbehavior

Do you speak before you listen carefully? (It's a perennial fault of us parents.) "Do not find fault before you investigate; first consider, and then reprove. Do not answer before you have heard, nor interrupt a speaker in the midst of his words" (Sirach 11:7–8). Did your child defy a command, or was the misbehavior an accident? Is he irresponsible, or did he genuinely forget? Be careful not to excuse whimsically nor accuse falsely. Differentiate between misunderstanding and noncompliance. Then correct misbehavior appropriately.

1. Instruction. Make pleasant but firm and reasonable requests. Give choices when you can. For instance, when dinner is ready and you call everyone, you can expect them to gather. However, some children adjust better with a five-minute warning before a change in activity. Just five minutes can help a child to complete a project or a part of it, clean up, and be ready for dinner. Such choices communicate respect for the child and assist him in obedience.

If your child is not defiant, use gentle physical manipulation to guide him toward obedience. When you can, make suggestions and offer explanations of good choices your child can make. Issue commands when necessary and appropriate, and warn with enforceable consequences. Caution against manipulative crying; while limited crying is allowed, angry protest crying is not. If your child's misbehavior goes unaddressed, it could become a defining characteristic. We correct gently but firmly.

Let your child know how much you value his feelings, individuality, opinions, and problem-solving abilities. You want to be approachable. If there is a problem, attack the problem —*not* the child. When your child claims things are different than they appear, risk believing him. You might even ask him what he thinks the punishment should be. Often my children recommend a more severe one than I think is just; I have the benefit of giving them (in their eyes) a lesser punishment. "Discipline your son, and he will give you rest; he will give delight to your heart" (Proverbs 29:17).

2. Natural consequences. Natural consequences are punishments directly related to the misbehavior. If a child dawdles and misses his ride for school, he has to pay bus fare himself. If he forgets his lunch, he has to buy lunch himself.

God corrected Israel with natural consequences: "In return for their foolish and wicked thoughts, which led them astray to worship irrational serpents and worthless animals, you sent upon them a multitude of irrational creatures to punish them, that they might learn that one is punished by the very things by which he sins" (Wisdom 11:15–16).

Connecting a deliberate misdeed to a natural consequence often makes the point.

3. Logical consequences. When natural consequences are too severe, logical consequences often suffice. If a child will not eat the dinner he served himself, should he sit until he can? Or should the punishment be that he forgo dessert that night and the next? A good rule is that food should not be wasted. If your child is full, however, you do not want him to overeat and be uncomfortable. Dessert is not necessary. Denying him a privilege reminds him how important it is to take smaller portions and finish the food he takes.

When our children refused to eat certain foods, we clarified our expectation. They had to take a small "No, thank you" helping and eat it without complaint. Apart from an occasional food that causes an involuntary gag reflex, like spinach, almost any food applied. This rule made for a more pleasant meal at home and when we visited others.

Another logical consequence might involve putting away a bike. Warn that an unlocked bike left outside may be stolen. If your child ignores your warning, rather than allowing the bike to be stolen (the severe natural consequence), bring it into the garage. Then tell him he has lost the privilege of biking for however long is reasonable.

4. Reinforcement. Reinforcement involves positive comments, justified praise, and a judicious use of rewards for good behavior. Sure, your child has to make his bed, but you can reinforce that habit by noticing and commenting on how neatly it was made or how orderly he is keeping his bedroom. Your praise can have even greater effect if you mention it in front of others.

My husband and I expect our children to do their schoolwork, but we offer rewards for extra credit work. We encourage a habit of saving money by offering our children, to a certain age, the incentive of doubling their deposits.

Finally, we try to catch them in the act of doing right. Many nights I wrangled with a child over bedtime. One evening I noticed he was in bed early, reading. I walked into his room and said, "I caught you."

His response was defensive. "It's not even my bedtime yet, but I'm in bed!"

I smiled. "Exactly. I caught you...doing right!" We both grinned.

5. *Time out.* Sometimes your child may try to manipulate you with protest crying, tantrums, sullen shyness, sulking, or a pity party of complaints. Removing your child from his audience may be effective. Send him to his room or sit him on a chair for a reasonable period of time. For children even five minutes can be long. If your child continues the behavior, increase the time or use another strategy.

One form of time out is the "I can" chair. When a child says, "I can't" do what is asked, refer him to the chair. "You will have to sit on the 'I can' chair until you can do what Mommy asks." It is amazing how quickly a child can have a change of heart—sometimes on the way to the chair. With the "I can" chair, a child is free as soon as the attitude changes.

Outside of our homeschool room we have stairs. When a child becomes emotional or noncompliant, I send him to the stairs to regain his composure. When he feels ready to rejoin us peacefully, he is welcomed.

One day Joe was annoyed. He announced, "I'm taking myself to the stairs. I'll be back when I'm not frustrated." It was a good move on his part, and he returned quickly.

6. Spanking. Spanking is limited to deliberately willful acts. Reasonable spanking without anger will not break the child's spirit. The goal is for the child to literally understand that consequences of sin are painful.

The punishment needs to fit the crime—not too lenient or too severe. Some people use a wooden spoon because it seems less personal—and less accessible—than a hand. One mother painted "Love me" on the spoon as a quick reminder to spank *only* as an act of love. Another mother shared that the time it took her to get the spoon helped her check her composure.

Many Proverbs recommend spanking. "He who spares the rod hates his son, but he who loves him is diligent to discipline him" (Proverbs 13:24). "Folly is bound up in the heart of a child, but the rod of discipline drives it far from him" (22:15).

Here is an acronym summarizing the important points of giving a spanking:

S: Spare the spirit; humiliation is not the goal.

P: Privately, not in public.

A: Ask the child to explain the disobedience first to be sure it was deliberate.

N: No anger on your part; if you are lacking control, wait.

K: Kiss, hold, and comfort the child afterward.

I: Instruct the child while he is teachable.

N: Necessary apologies and restitution from the child should follow.

G: Go in forgiveness; the punishment is over, and reconciliation has happened.

There is a crucial difference between hitting and spanking. Someone hits another person to hurt him or her. A parent spanks to help the child associate pain with disobedience and to deter future disobedience.

I want to offer a caveat: If physical abuse was a part of your upbringing and you fear repeating those errors in judgment, please do not spank. All discipline, including punishment, is to be an expression of love for the child.

7. Grounding. Grounding is a punishment that takes away "outside the home" privileges for anything other than school and obligations. It also prevents friends from coming over. Grounding is different from losing time with friends who are a poor influence or the privileges of biking or driving. Privileges can be lost if responsibilities are neglected, but that is not the same as grounding.

Grounding works for some parents, but I do not use it. Who really gets punished? Often it is the mom more than the child. The child mopes around looking for ways to communicate his frustration that he cannot go anywhere or do anything. Home becomes his prison. Though forgiveness presumably occurs right away, the punishment goes on and on.

I rarely meet the mom who can follow through with this punishment. Most kids know that if Mom says they are grounded for two days, it means one day; a week translates into a half week.

Caution regarding the love languages. Certain love languages increase a child's *sensitivity* to certain punishments. This does not rule out any particular punishment, but it is important to consider.

If your child's love language is words of affirmation, he may be sensitive to criticism. Watch your tone of voice and your words to avoid wounding his spirit with careless or cruel speech. Following the punishment, gently communicate how much you care about him.

If your child's love language is quality time, he may feel shunned by being sent to his room or a corner for an extended time. A brief sense of separation due to disobedience might strengthen his desire to obey, but emphasize your restored relationship afterward.

If your child's love language is gift giving, he might be sensitive to your taking away a toy or treat he was given. (Be careful not to give gifts with strings attached. Be sure your child understands a gift is really his before you require him to share it.) Let him know what needs to happen to get the gift back.

If your child's love language is acts of service, he may be sensitive to your rescinding a promise to do something for him. Yet it may be an appropriate consequence of his disobedience to withdraw an offer. Later you can offer another opportunity to fulfill that act of service.

If your child's love language is physical touch and closeness, he could be sensitive to painful physical touches. Suggestion: a firm "No" with a small smack on the hand may do more good in curbing bad behavior than a bottom spanking would on a different child. After the punishment confirm your reconciliation with physical affection.

OPENING A CHILD'S SPIRIT

Our goal as parents is to bend our child's will without breaking his spirit. Sometimes, however, we wound children's spirits when we discipline in anger, ignore their requests for help, or belittle them. Our harsh or careless words can make them feel ridiculed and disrespected. We discourage them with broken promises. "Hope deferred makes the heart sick, but a desire fulfilled is a tree of life" (Proverbs 13:12).

Miscommunication also causes a closed spirit in a child. If he perceives an injustice, through no fault of our own, he could react as if we intended harm. Whether real or perceived, a child's suffering can result in a broken relationship that will require our reaching out to him.

When a child closes his spirit to us, he also closes his mind, body, and will. He distances himself from us. He withholds affection or responds stiffly to our touch. He may become disrespectful, argumentative, or resistant to our requests. He may exhibit a contrarian spirit, choosing the opposite of our likes and dislikes, or embrace outright rebellion.

In order for our child to risk reopening his spirit to us, we have work to do. We pray for insight to make the relationship right, earnestly and humbly asking the Lord to show us our faults regardless of our child's faults. We may pursue spiritual direction in confession and counseling to gain objectivity about the situation.

We need to forgive our child, for our sake. When Jesus taught the Our Father, he warned, "For if you forgive men their trespasses, your heavenly Father also will forgive you; but if you do not forgive men their trespasses, neither will your Father forgive your trespasses" (Matthew 6:14–15). The Lord forgives us *as* we extend forgiveness to others! When we forgive someone, our wound begins to heal. When we refuse to forgive, our pain increases. What might not have been a mortal wound can become one.

How can we communicate genuine love and acceptance to this child? We pray for ways to fill our child's emotional bank in the hopes that he will be open to conversation. When he is willing to meet, we begin with being vulnerable—affirming our love for him, wanting to know how we have hurt him, and apologizing for causing him pain (the more specific, the better). This is risky. Asking for input does not mean we accept his assessment of our flaws—though he could be right—but we need to hear his heart.

We need to be tenderhearted toward our child, paying attention to his body language, facial expressions, and tone of voice. We want to speak genuine words of affirmation and encouragement. With prayer and effort our relationship can be restored.

Restoring Our Relationship

What if we have a closed spirit toward our child? It is painful to acknowledge, in the midst of conflict, that we cannot *feel* love for our child. It can be shattering to realize how imperfect we are as parents.

God is bigger than any problem we have, and he is available. He has greater love for our child than we will ever have; we ask him to place his love for our child in our heart.

Ponder the gift of this child. Think about the first time you held him—the feelings, the smell, the touch. Remember the hopes, prayers, and dreams you had for him. When I touched Joe for the first time, I remember finding words that captured my heart for each delivery: "You are the one I have loved all these months!"

The Lord wants to turn the hearts of parents to their children and children to their parents (see Malachi 4:6).

Sometimes we justify wrong actions, words, or thoughts because of the intensity of the pain of a broken relationship. We must ask God to reveal any sins we have committed against this child for which we have not repented. We let the Lord clear the debris caused by our sin so that he can reopen our heart to our child.

We also need the Lord to show us our child's true need. What is the root cause of our conflict? Are we struggling with each other because we are so different? Or are we too similar? Is there an outside influence? Or is there a conflict within our child?

We thank God for this child—yes, for *this* child, through whom God wants to do a great work of grace in our lives. How does he want us to pray? What does he want us to learn? What is he pruning in us?

Then let's imagine this child ten years from now. How different could things be? We believe God's grace can do a powerful work in our lives, and we pray for that. We then entrust this child to a particular saint, petitioning his guardian angel's assistance, and giving the relationship to the Holy Family, so that our family, like theirs, will reflect a civilization of love.

As the parent, you have the authority to speak the truth in love to your children. You have access to the grace you need to overcome your fears about parenting. You are obligated to continue the job you began. And remember, Jesus is the one who began this good work of parenting through you, and he will be faithful to complete it.

PART FIVE

She Opens

Her Mouth

With Wisdom

CHAPTER TWELVE

Making a Home for the Word

The Proverbs 31 woman "opens her mouth with wisdom, and the teaching of kindness is on her tongue" (verse 26). She teaches wisdom as she shares her faith with her children. Like this woman, we are called to teach our children the faith. Though many people can assist us, we are primarily responsible to catechize our children.

How are we qualified to teach our children the faith? We have four credentials: our vow, our marriage, our parenthood, and our call.

First, we vowed to accept children, should God bless us with them, and to raise them "according to the law of Christ and his Church."

Second, in addition to sacramental grace we receive regularly from confession and the Eucharist, we are strengthened for this task through our sacrament of holy matrimony.

Third, our natural love for our child motivates us. From the moment we first hold our child, we begin teaching him. How much more important is it to teach him the faith?

Fourth, God has called us to teach the faith to our children. "Parents have the first responsibility for the education of their children in the faith, prayer, and all the virtues" (*CCC*, 2252). In fact, Pope John Paul II wrote, "Their role as educators is so decisive that scarcely anything can compensate for their failure in it."[1] How can we teach the faith effectively?

Words and Deeds

How did Jesus learn the faith? Joseph and Mary catechized Jesus with their *words* and their *deeds*. They believed the angels' messages about the Messiah because they knew the prophecies. Mary declared the power and grace of God in her beautiful Magnificat (see Luke 1:46–55). Her prayer revealed a familiarity with Hannah's prayer (1 Samuel 2:1–10), in which Hannah glorified the Lord for exalting her as a humble servant through the gift of her son.

Mary knew the nighttime prayer that Jewish mothers taught their children, similar to "Now I lay me down to sleep, I pray the Lord my soul to keep…." She would have prayed over Jesus when he was a little boy, "Into your hand I commit my spirit" (Psalm 31:5a). Imagine her heart when, at the foot of the cross, she heard him utter it with the fullness of its meaning.

Joseph and Mary obeyed the law. They circumcised Jesus when he was eight days old. They presented him to God through Simeon in the temple and offered two turtledoves for the purification sacrifice when he was forty days old. They brought Jesus to Jerusalem for liturgical celebrations like Passover. Over time they witnessed Jesus' growth "in wisdom and in stature, and in favor with both God and man" (Luke 2:52). Mary and Joseph's yes to God's will was echoed in Jesus' words, "Your will be done" (Matthew 26:42b), in Gethsemane.

Likewise, Jesus catechized his disciples with his *words* and *deeds*. "And he went about all Galilee, teaching in their synagogues and preaching the gospel of the kingdom and healing every disease and every infirmity among the people"

(Matthew 4:23). Jesus taught his disciples how to pray and minister and then sent them to do what they had seen him do. "And preach as you go…. Heal the sick, raise the dead, cleanse lepers, cast out demons. You received without pay, give without pay" (Matthew 10:7a, 8).

With Jesus as a model, "parents are 'by word and example … the first heralds of the faith with regard to their children'" (*CCC*, 1656, quoting *Lumen Gentium*, 11). We cannot say we will live the faith rather than teach it; our lives are too imperfect. We also cannot teach the faith without living it, saying, "Do as I say, not as I do."

We have been called by God to lead our little ones to him. "Through the grace of the sacrament of marriage, parents receive the responsibility and privilege of *evangelizing their children*" (*CCC*, 2225). By baptizing our children we begin the process of their discipleship, but it does not end there. We are then called to teach them all that Jesus commanded, for "*raising children can be considered a genuine apostolate.*"[2]

Our lives, however imperfect, need to authenticate what we teach. "The Christian home is the place where children receive the first proclamation of the faith. For this reason the family home is rightly called 'the domestic church,' a community of grace and prayer, a school of human virtues and of Christian charity" (*CCC*, 1666). Like Saint Paul, we want to be able to say to our children, "What you have learned and received and heard and seen in me, do" (Philippians 4:9a).

We benefit from a good parish program that supports our teaching at home, since the parish is "a privileged place for the catechesis of children and parents" (*CCC*, 2226). However, we cannot expect the parish staff to substitute for us. We need to roll up our sleeves and explore the faith alongside our children, searching for answers with them. "Family catechesis therefore precedes, accompanies and enriches all other forms of catechesis."[3]

Jesus promises us his *presence* and his *power* to assist us in this monumental task. "In our own time, in a world often alien and even hostile to faith, believing families are of primary importance as centers of living, radiant faith" (*CCC*, 1656). To do this well we need to make a home for God's Word. How do we do that?

BUILD A SOLID FAMILY

In the Old Testament, *house* can refer to a family, like the phrase "the house of David," meaning David and his progeny. King David reminds us, "Unless the Lord builds the house, those who build it labor in vain" (Psalm 127:1a). We need the Lord to be the architect and builder of our family. He is the rock on which our house is built, so that when—not *if* but *when*—the storms of life come, we will still stand, together. "The wicked are overthrown and are no more, but the house of the righteous will stand" (Proverbs 12:7).

We do not want a family that *appears* solid but rather one that *is* solid. "By wisdom a house is built, and by understanding it is established; by knowledge the rooms are filled with all precious and pleasant riches" (Proverbs 24:3–4).

We begin with a solid foundation.

> So then you are no longer strangers and sojourners, but you are fellow citizens with the saints and members of the household of God, built upon the foundation of the apostles and prophets, Christ Jesus himself being the corner-

stone, in whom the whole structure is joined together and grows into a holy temple in the Lord; in whom you also are built into it for a dwelling place of God in the Spirit. (Ephesians 2:19–22)

Through our good works we build upon the foundation of Christ and the apostles.

Now if any one builds on the foundation with gold, silver, precious stones, wood, hay, straw—each man's work will become manifest; for the Day will disclose it, because it will be revealed with fire, and the fire will test what sort of work each one has done. (1 Corinthians 3:12–13)

Our roof, or our covering, is our consecration to the Lord. Shortly before his crucifixion Jesus prayed for his disciples, "And for their sake I consecrate myself, that they also may be consecrated in truth" (John 17:19). Jesus' consecration is our covering; our consecration is our family's covering—we are not leaving future generations out in the cold. The communion of persons in our family is a preparation for the communion of saints.

Jesus says, "Behold, I stand at the door and knock; if any one hears my voice and opens the door, I will come in to him and eat with him, and he with me" (Revelation 3:20). We invite Jesus into the interior home of our soul to dwell. And we welcome Jesus into the heart of our family to create a home for himself—the Word—with us.

FOCUS ON HEART AND SOUL

When a scribe asked Jesus to summarize the law, he quoted Deuteronomy 6:4–7:

> Hear, O Israel: The Lord our God is one Lord; and you shall love the Lord your God with all your heart, and with all your soul, and with all your might. And these words which I command you this day shall be upon your heart; and you shall teach them diligently to your children, and shall talk of them when you sit in your house, and when you walk by the way, and when you lie down, and when you rise. (See Mark 12:29–30)

The two most important tasks of parents are to love God wholeheartedly and to teach our children how to love God wholeheartedly. *How* are we to teach our children? Diligently. *When* are we to teach our children? Throughout the day. And *where* are we to teach them? Everywhere.

A wordless witness is not enough; we have to instruct. We need knowledge, the facts of the faith, and understanding, wisdom to know how to apply the faith. We educate the whole person for loving service for God—heart, soul, mind, and strength.

We want our children to know God intimately. It is not enough for a child to recite the Creed; we want him to believe it. More than simply listing the Ten Commandments, we want him to obey them. Beyond saying prayers, we want him to pray from the heart, whether by rote or extemporaneously.

From the moment we held our child for the first time, we cared for his physical needs. We fed him, clothed him, and cleaned him. Yet he has deeper needs than physical care—he has a soul that needs to be fed, clothed, and cleansed. "Fatherhood and motherhood represent a *responsibility which is not simply physical but spiritual in nature;* indeed, through these realities there passes the genealogy of the person, which has its eternal beginning in God and which must lead back to him."[4]

So we headed to the baptismal font. We brought him as a helpless infant and asked the Lord, through the ministry of the Church, to make him a child of God. We celebrated the fact that in Christ, he now has the grace of divine sonship and the gift of the Holy Spirit. This was not the end of our responsibility; it was the beginning of a new stage of growth.

Now we needed to nurture our child's new life in Christ. We looked for signs of faith in our children. During a tornado watch when we lived in Joliet, Illinois, our family went quickly to the basement for safety. Later our son Michael, then five, said, "It was like we were at church, and the Holy Spirit came like the wind. I threw open the doors, and I said, 'Come in! Come in!'"

When Jeremiah was six years old, he told me, "Mommy, I just prayed. I just became a total Christian. Are you a total Christian?" This was his language—not mine—but I assured him that yes, I was a total Christian, loving God with all my heart. Then he began asking about other family members: Were they total Christians? His young heart longed for everyone to have what he had. It was beautiful to see God at work, independent of us.

Children are spiritually sensitive, yet they do not always understand what we teach them. My grandniece Olivia thought the "Our Father" began with a question, "How do we know thy name?" Another child thought he prayed, "Howard be thy name." When our daughter was little, she led a decade of the rosary with the words "Hell, Mary," until we stopped her and explained to her the use of *Hail* as a word of greeting.

Teachable moments occur when we least expect them. For instance, Jeremiah, age seven, walked into the kitchen and asked me, "When does God sneeze?"

Before I could answer, Hannah chimed in, "God doesn't have a body. He doesn't sneeze." True enough, but there was more.

Scott joined the conversation. "Two thousand years ago he did. Jeremiah, do you remember how dusty it is in Israel? It was just as dusty when Jesus lived there. And I'm sure he sneezed. Since Jesus is fully God and fully man, you can say God sneezed."

Wow! In one brief conversation we covered God's being a spirit, Jesus' true humanity, and Jesus' humanity and divinity in the one Person of the Son. It was wonderful.

SAINT PAUL INSTRUCTS SAINT TIMOTHY

Though Saint Timothy's father was a Greek pagan, his mother, Eunice, and grandmother, Lois, instructed him in the Old Testament Scriptures. Their diligent teaching while he was a young boy laid the foundation for his faith in Christ (see 2 Timothy 3:14–15). Saint Paul wanted Saint Timothy to appreciate the continuity of what he had received as a child and how his faith was flourishing in Christ through the Scriptures. "All Scripture is inspired by God and profitable for teaching, for reproof, for correction, and for training in righteousness, that the man of God may be complete, equipped for every good work" (2 Timothy 3:16–17). Let's briefly examine the four areas delineated by Saint Paul as useful for our instruction.

Teaching refers to our doctrinal formation in the truths of the faith. Scripture is our primary, though not exclusive, text. "For whatever was written in former days was written for our instruction, that by steadfastness and by the encouragement of the Scriptures we might have hope" (Romans 15:4). We study Jesus' words and actions in the Gospels.

Pope John Paul II wrote, "To speak of Tradition and Scripture as the source of catechesis is to draw attention to the fact that catechesis must be impregnated and penetrated by the thought, the spirit and the outlook of the Bible and the Gospel through assiduous contact with the texts themselves."[5] We examine the mysteries of the faith by soaking in the Scriptures.

We have received *two gifts* with the Word of God. First, the Church affirms that the Bible is true. It is the words of God in the words of men. The same Holy Spirit who inspired God's Word preserves it from error; for God cannot lie. The Church urges Catholics to read the Bible privately and with the Church's liturgy, because the Word of God written is "strength for their faith, food for the soul, and a pure and lasting font of spiritual life" (*CCC*, 131). As Saint Paul says, "Let the word of Christ dwell in you richly" (Colossians 3:16a).

Second, the Holy Spirit was sent to lead the apostles into all truth (see John 16:13). The Spirit who inspired the Word preserves the Church's teaching from error. "First of all you must understand this, that no prophecy of Scripture is a matter of one's own interpretation, because no prophecy ever came by the impulse of man, but men moved by the Holy Spirit spoke from God" (2 Peter 1:20–21).

We will never exhaust the depths of knowledge about the faith, but we can enjoy the adventure of exploring the faith together with our children. We cannot give them what we do not have, but it is *never* too late to learn! Then we model a lifelong love of learning about the Lord.

One Thanksgiving we were traveling as a family to visit relatives. I had noticed that Joe had struggled with a religion lesson on the Person and natures of Christ. (It is challenging for anyone, let alone a fourth grader!) Scott used the opportunity to do a little *cartechesis* (catechesis in the car). He reviewed key concepts and then began asking Joe a series of questions. As Joe answered, our son David, then four, echoed.

"Joseph, is Jesus fully God?"

"Yes, he is," affirmed Joseph.

David chimed in, "Yes, he is!"

"Joseph, is Jesus fully man?"

"Yes, he is," Joseph answered confidently.

David acknowledged, "Yes, he is!"

"Joseph, is God eternal?" Scott asked.

Once again, Joseph stated clearly, "Yes, he is."

However, David emphatically said, "He is not!"

We were so surprised that we turned in our seats to understand what prompted such a strong response.

"David, why did you say God is not eternal?"

"I have seen a turtle; I know what a turtle is. And God is not a turtle!"

He was right, as far as he understood. With a little more instruction he understood more.

Two catechesis programs with outstanding materials have helped our family. "Catechesis of the Good Shepherd," by

Sophia Cavaletti, combines awareness of human development, respect for the spiritual sensitivities of a child, and a Montessori-type approach to teaching the child about the faith. "The Great Adventure," a comprehensive overview of salvation history, written by Jeff Cavins, now includes materials for children developed by his wife, Emily.

Reproof means to correct doctrinal errors and warn of their dangers, "so that we may no longer be children, tossed back and forth and carried about with every wind of doctrine, by the cunning of men, by their craftiness in deceitful wiles" (Ephesians 4:14). We cultivate a heart ready to respond to reproof. "Whoever hates reproof walks in the steps of the sinner, but he that fears the Lord will repent in his heart" (Sirach 21:6).

With every rosary we say the Apostles' Creed, and at every Sunday Mass we recite the Nicene Creed. From where did these creeds come? They were formulated and refined with great effort during debates at ecumenical councils. Sometimes fistfights broke out; sometimes holy men were exiled. Why?

Truth matters. This is the faith of our fathers. The more we understand why certain doctrines were formulated, the better equipped we will be for the theological battles of our day, many of which have already been fought and won.

Profitable for correction means that improper behavior is examined in light of the truth of God's Word. We cannot pick and choose which moral practices are true. As we study God's Word, we realize that all of us—adults and children— need to examine our behavior in light of God's standard.

Training in righteousness focuses on how we can grow in virtue and in holiness. Memorizing Scripture helps us. "How can a young man keep his way pure? By guarding it according to your word…. I have laid up your word in my heart, that I might not sin against you" (Psalm 119:9, 11). Protestants do not have a gene to make it easier to memorize Scripture, so no excuses from cradle Catholics that it is too difficult! Many people find it easier to memorize verses set to music.

Memorizing God's Word helps us to meditate when we do not have easy access to a Bible. We can review verses during a car pool or while working in the garden, taking a walk, or lying in bed. Twenty years ago on a family vacation, my dad shared his renewed commitment to memorize Scripture. In twenty years he has either memorized or rememorized more than one thousand verses. If you speak with him, you discover how many of them permeate his thoughts and words.

Knowledge by itself will not make us godly.

> For this very reason make every effort to supplement your faith with virtue, and virtue with knowledge, and knowledge with self-control, and self-control with steadfastness, and steadfastness with godliness, and godliness with brotherly affection, and brotherly affection with love. For if these things are yours and abound, they keep you from being ineffective or unfruitful in the knowledge of our Lord Jesus Christ. (2 Peter 1:5–8)

Knowledge supplemented with growth in virtue makes us spiritually fruitful.

WHY STUDY GOD'S WORD?

We study God's Word in order to be mature, equipped for every good work (see 2 Timothy 3:16–17). It is unlike any other sacred writing, "for the word of God is living and active, sharper than any two-edged sword, piercing to the division of soul and spirit, of joints and marrow, and discerning the thoughts and intentions of the heart" (Hebrews 4:12). When we share Scripture, we are able to speak God's words and not just give our own opinions. To share God's Word effectively, we need to study it carefully.

Saint Paul refers to the Word as the "sword of the Spirit" (Ephesians 6:17). (My nephews, who are Baptists, attended Bible memory clubs at their church, with "sword drills" for reviewing verses.) Why does Paul use such a vivid symbol that conjures images of battle, bloodshed, suffering, and victory or defeat?

> For though we live in the world we are not carrying on a worldly war, for the weapons of our warfare are not worldly but have divine power to destroy strongholds. We destroy arguments and every proud obstacle to the knowledge of God, and take every thought captive to obey Christ. (2 Corinthians 10:3–5)

We *are* in the midst of spiritual warfare. God's Word is an essential tool for each Christian disciple, adult or child, to know how to handle well. "Do your best to present yourself to God as one approved, a workman who has no need to be ashamed, rightly handling the word of truth" (2 Timothy 2:15).

We never know when we are going to need these truths at our fingertips. Memorizing verses helps us draw on the actual words rather than a vague concept in time of need. We experienced this firsthand on a vacation with our extended family.

Scott, the kids, and I were returning from Mass when we heard the siren. Somewhat casually we prayed for whoever needed help, until we saw my sister Kristi frantically waving the fire engine into the cul-de-sac where only our family stays. Immediately our prayer became an intense plea, "Oh, God, help! Help!"

When we arrived we realized the crisis was over. My nephew Stephen had almost drowned, but my sister Kari had saved his life. She had felt prompted to glance out of a bedroom window, and she saw our two-year-old nephew's body floating facedown in the pool. Racing through the house and down a flight of stairs, she leapt into the pool and came up under him. He immediately gasped for air.

My dad gathered us to pray over Stephen and his parents before they went to the hospital. After they left he turned to us and said, "Let's review our verse for the week: 'For to me to live is Christ, and to die is gain' (Philippians 1:21)."

I could barely choke out the words. Had Stephen died, it would have been better for him—God's Word was true—but it would have been devastating for us! This verse reminded us that death would not be the worst thing that could happen. Death apart from Christ would be. And for all of us— parents, spouses, siblings, and children—this verse renewed our resolve to live for Christ.

CHAPTER THIRTEEN

Living Witnesses: Sharing the Faith in Our Family

J esus taught his disciples how to pray by praying with them, for them, and apart from them. We follow his example with our own children. Pope John Paul II wrote,

> The concrete example and living witness of parents is fundamental and irreplaceable in educating their children to pray. Only by praying together with their children can a father and mother—exercising their royal priesthood—penetrate the innermost depths of their children's hearts and leave an impression that the future events in their lives will not be able to efface.[1]

This includes our habits of family prayer as well as moments of spontaneous prayer as the need arises.

I needed prayer. I was in a panic: In thirty minutes I would be addressing fifteen hundred people at Franciscan University, and my talk had not gelled. I spotted Jeremiah, then six years old, in our front hallway and said, "Honey, please pray for Mommy. I'm not ready to give this talk."

Immediately he put his hand up and his head down and began to pray. I didn't have time for this prayer, but I had asked him to pray. I dropped to my knees, and his hand rested on my head. His prayer was simple but beautiful. Then he hugged me. I was on my way with the perfect illustration to conclude my talk. But even more, my heart was filled with gratitude that my little boy was my brother in Christ.

Children are spiritually sensitive. They respond when we read Bible stories and sing songs about Jesus. They listen when we hold them at Mass and whisper what each part means. They draw near for a blessing before bed (sometimes with holy water). They know God's love initially through our love for them. As our children mature, we witness God touching their lives directly, guiding and calling them in unique ways.

HABITS OF PRAYER THROUGHOUT THE DAY

Most school mornings Scott gathers our family for prayer. We consecrate the day to the Lord using a Morning Offering. We read the Gospel of the day, the life of the saint for that day, and facts about a country for which we will pray. Then we pray for our family's needs and others' concerns with extemporaneous prayers, youngest to oldest. We close with an Our Father, Hail Mary, and the Guardian Angel and Saint Michael prayers. We huddle together, and Scott prays a blessing over us. What a great start to the day!

If we are attentive, opportunities to pray come throughout the day: before meals, in the car for safety, and when needs arise. We make the Sign of the Cross when we go by churches and cemeteries. Even a child under two can signal the family that a siren is sounding, so that we pause to pray for whoever is in need.

After dinner we routinely shift to more comfortable seats and pray a rosary. "Because of Mary's singular cooperation with the action of the Holy Spirit, the Church loves to pray in communion with the Virgin Mary, to magnify with her the great things the Lord has done for her, and to entrust supplications and praises to her" (*CCC*, 2682). I love to contemplate the mysteries and unite my prayers for my children, godchildren, and grandchildren with the virtues each mystery highlights.[2]

Before bed we bless the children with a special prayer: "May the grace of our Lord Jesus Christ, and the love of God the Father, and the communion of the Holy Spirit be with you now and forever 'til we're in heaven together. Amen."

PRAYING THE MASS

Sunday is a special opportunity to pray the Mass with your children. *Never* substitute CCD for Mass or send your children to Mass alone. It is serious sin to miss Sunday Mass intentionally, and your children need to participate with you.

Young children can and should be trained to participate at Mass. Realize that it takes time and patience to train them. Briefly remove a child when he is disruptive, even if the sound he makes is the enjoyable echo of his voice off the high ceiling. (It may feel like a "walk of shame," but it is not.) For the sake of elderly people struggling to hear and the priest trying to preach, leave intending to return as soon as you can. This is part of training a child.

If your parish offers a "quiet" room for children, please do not make it a place for toys and snacks. It should be a place to quiet your child, and then you should return to the congregation. Some "quiet" rooms are so full of adults and older children that parents who really need the space cannot find a place to sit.

Older congregants need to be patient with younger parents, who need our support and encouragement, not glares! Remember Jesus' words, "Let the children come to me, do not hinder them; for to such belongs the kingdom of God" (Mark 10:14b). One Sunday my mom approached a young mother and said, "Your baby reminded me what I sound like to God." What a great perspective! There is a place for everyone near Jesus.

Since each Sunday is a mini-Easter celebration, we have a special dinner at home. Even our older children who attend college join us most Sundays for a special feast, using china and silver, to highlight the first-day-of-the-week observance of our Lord's resurrection. (It has been a wonderful way to get to know Sarah and Ana, who married our sons Gabriel and Michael.)

Weekday Masses help with training because they are shorter than Sunday Masses. They provide reminders between Sundays; children who go to Mass only once a week may forget what is expected of them. The years are few in which we can decide our children will attend daily Mass; I do not want to miss the opportunity. When complaints are heard—yes, even in the Hahn household—I begin (and they chime in), "We don't *have* to go to Mass: We *get* to!"

Daily Mass is not obligatory, but frequent attendance at Mass demonstrates to our children our priority to be with Jesus in the midst of our busy day. It provides a rhythm of receiving our Lord and giving ourselves to him. For me it is a time of reconnecting my work to the eternal reasons I labor: It is all for Jesus.

We bring our children to Jesus, who heals hearts, strengthens resolve, and calls them to holiness. We take older children with us for visits to the Blessed Sacrament or encourage them to sign up for their own holy hour. Once they can drive they can take a sibling. One of our local parishes offers "Children of Hope" Holy Hours that are specifically geared for training young children in Eucharistic adoration.[3]

THE LITURGICAL CALENDAR IN OUR HOME

Each year we observe the mysteries of Christ's incarnation, life, death, resurrection, and ascension and anticipate his second coming. This provides a cycle of fasting and feasting in our home according to the liturgical calendar. We have enjoyed reading about others' traditions and deciding what ours will be.

We observe the penitential seasons of Advent and Lent as we prepare for Christmas and Easter feasts. Here are a few ideas.

For Advent a friend noted that fire (Advent wreath candles) and sugar (cookies shaped with nativity cookie cutters) keep the children's attention. When children do kind deeds throughout Advent, they add a straw to soften Jesus' manger. For Christmas they have a birthday cake for Jesus.

For Lent one family places thorns in a wreath; children remove a thorn for each good deed they do, placing the thorn in a jar. For Easter the jar filled with thorns is replaced by a jar filled with jelly beans. And the beans' colors are given a special meaning: Black refers to our sin; red to Jesus' blood; white to us in Christ.

We appreciate learning special ways to celebrate holy days. This can be a great topic of conversation, a way of gleaning tried and tested ideas from others. We also celebrate our patron saint feast days and baptismal anniversaries in special ways.

We prepare the children for receiving sacraments and celebrate with them. Besides the usual celebrations of First Communion and confirmation, we celebrate our children's first confession by all going to confession the same night and then getting ice cream afterward. ("Children must go to the sacrament of penance before receiving Holy Communion for the first time" [*CCC*, 1456, quoting canon 914].)

All sins harm the communion of the family; all acts of charity build up the family. "Do nothing from selfishness or conceit, but in humility count others better than yourselves. Let each of you look not only to his own interests, but also to the interests of others" (Philippians 2:3–4). We encourage going to confession regularly and receiving the Eucharist frequently, not only for their good but to strengthen our whole family.

Try not to feel overwhelmed by all of the wonderful suggestions. You cannot do them all. Ask yourself, will this idea help our family this year, or will it be burdensome? We want to please the Lord and our family, not succumb to peer pressure to prove how orthodox we are. We can still be creative and adjust our expectations to what is best for our family each year. For outstanding resources, I recommend *Faith and Family Magazine*,[4] and the Holy Heroes' Advent Adventure, Lenten Adventure, and Summer Adventure, available free online.[4]

CONSECRATING OUR HOME

We highly recommend asking a priest to bless your home; he will also bless an apartment! There is a special consecration of the family to the lordship of Christ called the Enthronement of the Sacred Heart.[6] It has its own brief liturgy to dedicate your home and your lives to the Lord. Each year, at the Feast of the Epiphany, you can also receive blessed chalk to mark the doorways into your home for the new year.[7]

Religious art nourishes faith by enkindling love for Jesus, Mary, and the saints, much like a wall of family photos. The goal is not a pious wallpapering of images but some beautiful pieces that draw your hearts to think about the Lord throughout the day. Perhaps a painting needs to be rematted or reframed so that it blends with the style of your decorating. Take time to select the art that will inspire contemplation.

HARMONY IN OUR HOME

We are capable of great good or harm with our words. Saint James offers several word-pictures to illustrate just how powerful our tongues are:

> If we put bits into the mouths of horses that they may obey us, we guide their whole bodies. Look at the ships also; though they are so great and are driven by strong winds, they are guided by a very small rudder wherever the will of the pilot directs. So the tongue is a little member and boasts of great things. How great a forest is set ablaze by a small fire! (James 3:3–5)

Just as a horse's gait and direction are altered by the bit and bridle in his mouth, or a ship's direction is altered by its rudder, so our tongues guide the direction of conversations and relationships. James likens the power of a tongue to fire. Just as massive forests can be destroyed by just a few flames, so our careless words can do great harm.

We can influence both the physical and spiritual health of those we love by choosing our words wisely. "The mind of the wise makes his speech judicious, and adds persuasiveness to his lips. Pleasant words are like a honeycomb, sweetness to the soul and health to the body" (Proverbs 16:23–24). We want to speak with wisdom. "To make an apt answer is a joy to a man, and a word in season, how good it is!" (Proverbs 15:23).

We can contribute much to the harmony of our home—and so can our children—depending on our speech. Let's examine some of the central ideas about godly use of our tongues here. "There is gold, and abundance of costly stones; but the lips of knowledge are a precious jewel" (Proverbs 20:15). Appendix D lists more Scriptures to examine.

Words reveal the heart. The Pharisees taught that eating certain foods made the people unclean. Jesus addressed the deeper issue: "Hear and understand: not what goes into the mouth defiles a man, but what comes out of the mouth, this defiles a man.... But what comes out of the mouth proceeds from the heart, and this defiles a man" (Matthew 15:10b–11, 18). His words echo the proverb, "Keep your heart with all vigilance; for from it flow the springs of life" (Proverbs 4:23).

Jesus clarified:

> For out of the abundance of the heart the mouth speaks. The good man out of his good treasure brings forth good, and the evil man out of his evil treasure brings forth evil. I tell you, on the day of judgment men will render account for every careless word they utter; for by your words you will be justified, and by your words you will be condemned. (Matthew 12:34b–37)

Even our careless words will be judged.

If we are taking God's Word seriously, our actions have to match our words. "If any one thinks he is religious, and does not bridle his tongue but deceives his heart, this man's religion is vain" (James 1:26). Christ's word in our hearts will change our hearts, if we "let the word of Christ dwell in [us] richly" (Colossians 3:16a).

Form habits that can grow into virtues. Our tongues get us—adults *and* children—into a lot of trouble, especially when we lack control of our emotions. "Emotions and feelings can be taken up into the *virtues* or perverted by the *vices*" (*CCC*, 1768). We cannot help feeling emotion; we can decide to use self-control. "When words are many, transgression is not lacking, but he who restrains his lips is prudent" (Proverbs 10:19).

Sometimes we give in to self-pity when we are sick. Instead of criticizing his brother, I overheard one son say to another, "Can you offer up your flu for someone who needs prayer?"

With barely a pause this sick little one bowed his head and offered his pain "for a woman somewhere who is thinking about having an abortion." I brushed away tears at his simple yet remarkable heart for someone he did not know. I was so grateful to his brother for guiding him to an expression of sacrifice over self-pity.

Words can cut like a sword or a scalpel. Sometimes we have to say something that will be difficult for someone else to hear. "There is one whose rash words are like sword thrusts, but the tongue of the wise brings healing" (Proverbs 12:18). How we say the truth matters, but we must always tell the truth. "Lying lips are an abomination to the LORD, but those who act faithfully are his delight" (Proverbs 12:22).

Men and women struggle with different aspects of fanning the flames of conflict. Insubordinate men stir up strife with false teaching (see Titus 1:10–11); idle women spread gossip (see 1 Timothy 5:13). We should avoid men and women who engage in this kind of conflict. "He who goes about gossiping reveals secrets; therefore do not associate with one who speaks foolishly" (Proverbs 20:19).

Respect for others includes guarding their reputations, whether or not an accusation could be true. We should avoid rash judgments that someone has sinned (see *CCC*, 2477) and not share negative information about someone, true or false, with someone who does not need to know.

> In these you once walked, when you lived in them. But now put them all away: anger, wrath, malice, slander, and foul talk from your mouth. Do not lie to one another, seeing that you have put off the old man with his practices and have put on the new man, who is being renewed in knowledge after the image of his creator. (Colossians 3:7–10)

We want our words to strengthen others, in imitation of our heavenly Father.

God's words are life-giving; ours can be as well. "The tongue of the wise dispenses knowledge, but the mouths of fools pour out folly…. A gentle tongue is a tree of life, but perverseness in it breaks the spirit" (Proverbs 15:2, 4). We can quell a quarrel: "For lack of wood the fire goes out; and where there is no whisperer, quarrelling ceases" (Proverbs 26:20).

We must think before we speak. "Let your speech always be gracious, seasoned with salt, so that you may know how you ought to answer every one" (Colossians 4:6). Further, we do not have to say everything we think. "He who restrains his words has knowledge, and he who has a cool spirit is a man of understanding" (Proverbs 17:27). We ask the Lord to help us use restraint, "Set a guard over my mouth, O LORD, keep watch over the door of my lips!" (Psalm 141:3).

Since we want to plant the seeds of faith rather than the weeds of cynicism, we never speak poorly about priests or bishops. If there are problems we as adults need to address, we do so privately. We discourage a judgmental spirit toward those in spiritual authority over us. "Finally, brethren, whatever is true, whatever is honorable, whatever is just, whatever is pure, whatever is lovely, whatever is gracious, if there is any excellence, if there is anything worthy of praise, think about these things" (Philippians 4:8). As a pastor, my father honored those who exercised authority in our church. I am grateful that he protected our hearts from a critical spirit toward our spiritual leaders.

IT'S NOT TOO LATE

It is never too late to live the faith well in your marriage and family life. Today is a time to renew your commitment to communicate God's grace with your words.

God wants to build a home within you and me—a temple for him—so that the faith flourishes in our lives. He also wants to establish our home as a place that honors him by our words and deeds. "As therefore you received Christ Jesus the Lord, so live in him, rooted and built up in him and established in the faith, just as you were taught, abounding in thanksgiving" (Colossians 2:6–7).

PART SIX

The Teaching

of Kindness Is on

Her Tongue

CHAPTER FOURTEEN

Sculpting a Life Through Education at Home

To sculpt a statue takes time, thought, planning, and careful work. "To 'sculpt' a life, in the midst of life itself," says Edith Schaeffer, "takes more work, is for longer periods of time, and needs far more patience."[1] As Pope Pius XII wrote, "[M]others ... exert the earliest and the most intimate influence upon the souls of little ones and upon their growth in piety and virtue.... [s]urely no art is more difficult and strenuous than that of fashioning the souls of children."[2]

To parent is to teach. Pope John Paul II wrote, "*Parents* are *the first and most important educators* of their own children, and they also possess a *fundamental competence* in this area: they are *educators because they are parents*."[3] This chapter focuses on a mother's influence as the primary educator of her children. "The teaching of kindness is on her tongue" (Proverbs 31:26b). Like the woman of Proverbs 31, we want to teach with wisdom and kindness.

Our goal is to educate the whole person. We integrate the knowledge of our faith with character formation, academic training, and development of life skills. Education "is a living means of communication, which not only creates a profound relationship between the educator and the one being educated, but also makes them both sharers in truth and love,

173

that final goal to which everyone is called by God the Father, Son and Holy Spirit."[4]

What a beautiful picture of what education can be.

OUR CHOICE TO HOMESCHOOL

When our oldest children were quite young, Scott and I began reading about homeschooling. We were impressed with homeschoolers' academic scores. We were intrigued by the variety of methods, styles, and curricula available. We could have really smart kids! Then we realized that just as our goal for our children should not be either beauty or brawn, so it also should not be brains.

There are, after all, brilliant atheists in the world. They have knowledge but do not place it in service to the One who created them. "'Knowledge' puffs up, but love builds up" (1 Corinthians 8:1b). We want to train their hearts *and* their minds: godliness *and* excellent academic training. Our educational goal for our children has been and continues to be that they be self-directed, lifelong learners who serve the Lord with their gifts, abilities, skills, and knowledge.

The Principle of Subsidiarity

The principle of subsidiarity, applied to education, means "[w]henever the family is self-sufficient, it should be left to act on its own."[5] We can delegate to either a private or public school, as necessary for the well-being of each child, provided the school is accountable to us as parents. Homeschooling has been a wonderful option for our family.[6]

Through prayer and conversation with your spouse, you will discern the best educational choice for your children. Since you may not be familiar with homeschooling, I want to share some of the information that helped us consider that choice. I do not think homeschooling is the only choice for Christians, but it is an excellent option, especially for learning and living the faith in a vibrant way as a family.

Advantages of Homeschooling

Love and authority. A homeschooling parent does what any good teacher would like to do: Combine unconditional love for her child with her natural authority. I tell my son, "You are my favorite fourth-grader!" A parent chooses the curricula she likes the best—no committee approval needed.

The value of tutoring. If a child struggles with concepts, one-on-one instruction is usually recommended. Why? Tutoring is *the* most efficient form of education. A tutor immediately knows if the child understands. The tutor can alter the educational approach, based on the child's style of learning. If the difficulty lies with the curriculum, a tutor can select a different text. The focus remains teaching the child, not the curriculum.

The goal is understanding. In homeschooling you teach for mastery of material, not grades. Grades are a necessary shortcut for teachers in classrooms to assess the progress of many children. A homeschooling parent knows how the child is doing.

Go at the child's pace. What is your child's readiness and developmental stage? If he is ready to read, great. If not, you work on identifying letters and their sounds. If he is ready to do math, great. If not, you teach concepts about patterns by working with manipulatives.

The first day of our second homeschool year, Gabriel, then four, was in tears. He expected to start school and was disappointed that I had planned for him to wait. Since he was so eager, I found him some kindergarten books, and we began.

Gabriel worked with the letter *b*, and then he did math, page after page, for hours. I tried to shelve the book, but he begged me to let him do more. After five hours he had completed half of the book, and I told him, much to his dismay, he had to put it down. The next day he learned *d* and then completed the kindergarten math book. On day three Gabriel worked on *f* and began the first-grade math book.

Though he excelled at math, he could not combine letters to read; it did not make sense to him. So we played with letters for the rest of the year, and he worked on math to his heart's content. At the end of the year, he said his favorite subject was learning letters! Had he attended school, he would have been bored with math and probably labeled a failure in reading, which happily never happened.

The next year Gabriel easily put letters together to make words, and he continued his prowess in math. Year after year he did fine in reading, but he excelled in math, completing calculus at age fourteen. He took Calculus I, II, and III at Franciscan University before he was eighteen and then majored in math. He might be particularly gifted, or perhaps he had the opportunity to develop his natural ability.

Each of my children has discovered a subject in which he or she excelled, be it English, history, writing, or math. Homeschooling enabled them to explore their area of interest while maintaining the other subjects.

When Jeremiah took a long time to learn to read, I did not

panic. I knew that children develop at different rates. I tried different methods and readers. Once the developmental adjustment occurred, reading made sense to him. Though he was nearly nine when he learned to read, Jeremiah became my best reader by age ten. He would sit for hours and enjoy encyclopedias, history books, and mythology. What a blessing that he did not feel like a failure when he was younger. He just needed time to mature.

Avoid the fear of failure. The homeschooled child is always succeeding because understanding is the goal. If he struggles with math or reading, he is not separated into a group that other children know is the "dumb" group (for example, blue birds versus robins). The child also does not fear criticism or ridicule from other students when he or she struggles.

Avoid the fear of misunderstanding assignments. A homeschooled child receives immediate feedback on his performance. If there are errors, he can correct them right away. If he is unsure of the assignment, he is not afraid to ask questions.

Avoid boredom. Many bright children, though not ignored, are not adequately challenged in a typical classroom. In homeschooling time is well spent—not wasted on busywork. If a child understands a concept, he does not have to do more pages to keep him occupied; he goes on to the next concept. If a child does not understand a concept, he focuses on it until he understands it.

Delight-directed learning considers the child's unique personality, gifts, and interests. Since homeschool tutoring takes much less time than regular classroom instruction, a child has more time to explore interests, learn an instrument, develop friendships, or work on a hobby or sport.

I am so grateful for the opportunity I have had to teach my children for more than twenty years. And if my grandchildren live in the area, I may offer my services!

Other miscellaneous benefits. Homeschooling allows flexibility in your schedule. You can take field trips whenever you want, whereas many school districts have cancelled field trips because of the cost of gas and the lack of parent chaperones. A sick child does not fall behind; when he is well you resume the assignments. If Dad works swing shift, you can adjust the school schedule so that you have more family time. If you have an occasional late night, you can adjust the school schedule. If you want to take a trip, you can take school on the road.

Since you tutor, your school year is shorter; it takes fewer hours than a typical school day. When people ask if my kids get snow days, I say, "No, they get sun days, since we finish in early May." We also do a small amount of summertime schooling to keep reading and math skills fresh, so that we do not waste time in the fall.

You will have healthier children since they are not mixing germs with a classroom of children. You do not have to wake a baby to drive a carpool. And if the weather is bad, you do not have to go outside.

You can offer an excellent education at a fraction of the cost of a private school. If you purchase nonconsumable materials, the price diminishes with each additional child who uses them. You can even lend them to others the years you do not need them.

Instead of scattering people in many directions, homeschooling unifies the family. You can plan your school day around devotions and sacraments. You spend the best hours of the day together. You work on schoolwork when you have the most energy, instead of in the late afternoon or evening when you are all tired. You enjoy a quantity of quality time, and when you complete schooltime, there is no homework to do.

Can You Homeschool?

Homeschooling is *not* the only choice for authentic Catholic families, but it is an excellent option for you to consider. You have already done the hard work: You have taught them to walk, talk, and go to the bathroom properly. Now you have the pleasure of seeing their minds and hearts grasp knowledge of life and the world. You have been homeschooling by virtue of being a parent; this is just more structured, with set goals, a plan, and curriculum.

It is not a question of being totally self-sufficient for the job but being available to do whatever God calls you to do. If he is calling you to this, he will give you the grace to do it. Unity with your spouse in this calling of homeschooling is essential.

No one is born a teacher, though some people are by nature more nurturing. The desire to teach plus great resources produce great educators. You will find that anyone is willing to sell curricula to a homeschooler—public, private, and homeschool sources. Teacher guides are available with detailed lesson plans; books are available from the library to help you cut curricular costs. Local and national support groups as well as homeschool teaching support companies provide everything from encouragement to prepackaged grade-level materials that include grading and testing services.

Homeschooling provides a great opportunity to model for your children that learning is lifelong. You can learn alongside your child subjects you may not have understood when you were in school, like geography, fractions, the Renaissance, or the human body.

Though you will want to accomplish many educational goals, remember that you are a mom who is teaching her little ones and not a drill sergeant who adds mothering. Direct the child toward maturity with compassion, respect, and charity. You have the love to motivate you to bring out the best in them, to challenge them to be all they can while knowing their limits. Your integration of education with all phases of child training will bear fruit for years to come for your child and your family.

Instill Values—Yours!

Your child's education should reflect your values. Public schools tend to erect barriers between Christian values and subject matter. The faith may not be attacked directly, but it can be treated as something private, with little relevance in the sphere of knowledge. By compartmentalizing a child's spiritual development, teachers give the impression that faith does not apply when discussing the facts of school subjects. But faith and knowledge go together.

God is the source of all knowledge, not just religious knowledge. Parochial schools have been built on this premise for the good of all students, Christian or not, who attend. This is also the assumption of Catholic homeschooling.

Unfortunately, all Catholic schools are not faithful to this vision. Their curricular choices and spiritual guidance of students may reflect the culture as much as do public schools. The only difference may be that parents are paying extra for the malformation of their children. Only too late have some families discovered that their children were so poorly formed in the faith that they no longer chose to live Christian lives when they graduated. Parents need to remain vigilant about their children's instruction when they delegate it to a school claiming to be Catholic.

Socialization

One aspect of character development is socialization. Often people think schools are the obvious choice for socializing children. Consider the following thoughts.

Socialization is typically reduced to sociability among peers. The goal is conformity. Children who are smart or talented can suffer from consequences of jealousy and envy. All behavior cannot be monitored. Unkind conduct or vulgar conversations on the playground, in the locker room, or in the cafeteria can expose a child to harmful words and actions. Metal detectors reduce incidences of children bringing weapons to school, but physical harm still occurs. Many teachers and administrators are hampered by the fear of lawsuits in their attempts to exert authority to deal with bad behavior.

What is the purpose of socialization? Is it not learning the lifelong skill of how to function in the body of Christ and in society? Specifically, do our children know how to respond to authority without a critical spirit, so they can be good followers? Do they have the skills to lead others faithfully as servant-leaders? Are they aware of needs around them, and do they care for others? Do they handle negative peer pressure well and encourage peers for good? "He who walks with wise men becomes wise, but the companion of fools will suffer harm" (Proverbs 13:20).

When you talk about healthy social growth, a school setting has limitations. It is an artificial environment where peers are segregated. Home, on the other hand, provides the natural environment with age integration that you find in the neighborhood, at your parish, and at work. Home provides socialization for life.

Home is not an escape from the real world: There is plenty of sin in our homes. However, training is begun, nurtured, sustained, repaired, and matured under the watchful care of parents. Our training does not always have the desired effect, but we keep trying.

One school morning Hannah, then age seven, was irritable. I wanted her to focus on being thankful. I asked her to leave the room until she could return with a list of things for which she was thankful.

I knew we were in trouble when she entered the room, still looking disgruntled, and announced she would read her list aloud. "I thank God I am none of the following." I took a deep breath, trying not to smile. She read each word slowly with a dramatic pause: "bald, homeless, an idiot, earless, dead, selfish, shy, terrible, or stupid." We laughed until we cried, which did not have a happy effect on Hannah. She had obeyed the letter of the law but not the spirit of it.

In training in social skills, sheer numbers of children in large classes may be more hindrance than help. Regardless of teachers' desires to refine children's characters, parents cannot expect that of teachers: There is too little time. But parents can fine-tune character training. They can deal with a child's lack of kindness, unwillingness to serve others, or boasting, for example.

At the same time, the virtue of friendship needs to be fostered between our children and like-minded friends. A wonderful activity group combining social time for girls and their moms with growing in the faith and character development is Little Flowers Girls' Club.[7] Girls five and older gather to learn about the faith and study saints that correspond to one of nine virtues. They earn badges (petals of a flower) throughout the year. Their meetings involve Scripture memory, crafts, catechism, activities, and service projects.

There are other girls' and boys' programs that focus on developing character in the context of learning the faith. Kids for Jesus[8] is for children in the third to eighth grades. For these same grade levels, Challenge Clubs[9] for girls and Conquest Clubs[10] for boys also provide leadership opportunities in apostolate in addition to teaching and applying the faith. These groups encourage positive peer relationships in the context of having fun and growing in faith. And they in turn strengthen families.

Home is like a greenhouse. It provides a place for healthy social growth without the harsher elements of the outside world. The goal is transplantation at the right time, according to the parents' discernment.

> The family is the first and fundamental school of social living: as a community of love, it finds in self-giving the law that guides it and makes it grow. The self-giving that

inspires the love of husband and wife for each other is the model and norm for the self-giving that must be practiced in the relationships between brothers and sisters and the different generations living together in the family. And the communion and sharing that are part of everyday life in the home at times of joy and at times of difficulty are the most concrete and effective pedagogy for the active, responsible and fruitful inclusion of the children in the wider horizon of society.[11]

Ordinary life at home, lived in the context of faith, prepares our children to know how to function well in society while living faithfully for the Lord.

If *you* are social, *your children* will be social. Friendships are built on common experiences—learning together, working together, serving together. You can make that possible. *Stay involved* no matter how your child is educated. Get to know the teachers and the curricula; know what your children's activities are, and meet their friends. Remember: Quality time together as a family encourages good social skills.

CHAPTER FIFTEEN

Training in Practical Life Skills

athers and mothers are teachers of life for life. We follow the example of the Proverbs 31 mother, who teaches her children *with kindness* (see Proverbs 31:26). We gently train our children to contribute to the family with increasing responsibilities. We help them develop inner discipline, self-respect, and a sense of teamwork. The *Catechism* affirms, "The home is the natural environment for initiating a human being into solidarity and communal responsibilities" (*CCC*, 2224).

THE VALUE OF MANNERS

We teach our children social graces. We teach them table manners to make meals more pleasant at home and when they eat with others. We train them to serve the family at meals so that hosting guests goes smoothly.

We teach them how to answer the phone and how to greet someone at the front door. We help them practice introductions, so that they are comfortable meeting people they do not know. Our training in etiquette enables our children to interact socially more easily.

THE VALUE OF WORK

I am often asked, how can you homeschool and complete your housework? Simple. My children are part of my work crew. They help my efforts rather than hinder them. Our shared labors enable us to accomplish school *and* have a well-ordered home.

As mothers we do not give our children chores to avoid doing work. We set an example by doing our housework well. Plus we reinforce the beauty and dignity of manual labor as we train them to assist us. "Whatever your task, work heartily, as serving the Lord and not men, knowing that from the Lord you will receive the inheritance as your reward; you are serving the Lord Christ" (Colossians 3:23–34).

How can children help? Between the ages of two and three, a child can help with simple tasks. He can make his bed, help you make other beds, put away toys, put dirty clothes in a hamper, or throw away trash. In the kitchen he can clean fruits and vegetables, tear lettuce, shuck corn, spread butter on toast, and knead dough.

Between the ages of four and seven, a child can set the table, collect trash, care for pets, collect and sort laundry, and do simple yard work. In the kitchen he can crack eggs, stir pitchers of juice, measure things, and help with cooking and baking. We offer an allowance at these ages (forty cents a week at age four, fifty cents a week at five, sixty cents a week at six, seventy cents a week at seven) until they begin budgeting at age eight (see my next section). We teach them to tithe 10 percent, which they place in the offering basket at church, and to save 10 percent in their piggy banks. The rest they can spend.

Routine helps a child remember to do chores. Set daily chores for the same time each day; weekly chores for the same time each week, like yard work on Saturday mornings, for example. This simplifies your supervision when it involves more than one child.

One friend in the neighborhood acknowledged she has chores for her children that, of course, they do not like. She told my son, with a smile, "I am the 'meanest mom' around." Our goal is not to be their best friend right now but their parent. We have years to be the greatest of friends once they have grown.

THE VALUE OF MONEY MANAGEMENT

One of the most liberating ideas in parenting that my husband and I have found is developing budgets with our children. We have adapted principles from Ron and Judy Blue's book *Money Matters for Parents and Their Kids* (Oliver-Nelson, 1988). Here is how we have made it work for our family. Feel free to adjust the program to fit your family—we did! Please do not be concerned if you are not a math person (my daughter's advice). See Appendix B for a step-by-step checklist to minimize confusion.

Begin at age eight! (I know—eight?) Children rise to the occasion beautifully, though they need guidance. They develop character while learning financial management with increasing responsibilities and rewards. At age eight they provide 5 percent of the budget; by age eighteen they provide 100 percent. (Budgets for college will be addressed in my next book.)

Before you begin, identify which personal chores each child will continue to have for which there will be no pay. These chores help them contribute to family life. In our family they include daily hygiene, putting clothes away, doing schoolwork, making their beds, picking up their bedrooms, and completing a dish duty.

Step One. You and your child choose his budget categories. For the most part these are items for which you are already spending money. Categories may include clothes, a coat, shoes, sports, haircuts or hair care products (beyond what you would normally purchase), Boy Scouts (or another activity with expenses), books, music or art lessons, personal spending, gifts, long-term savings, and tithe.

Step Two. Determine the budget per category. Over the next six months, what will the child need? (We revise our budgets every six months.) What should he budget on a monthly basis to meet those needs? You may want to begin after the eighth birthday or Christmas, so that you know he already has the clothes, coat, shoes, and so on that he needs right then. The budget provides for future rather than immediate needs in these areas.

EXAMPLE A:	*Partial Monthly Budget*
Coat	$5.00
Clothing	$20.00
Shoes	$7.50
Haircut	$7.50
Books	$2.00
Sports	$10.00
Personal allowance	$8.00
Long-term savings	10 percent
Tithe	10 percent
Subtotal	$60.00 (excluding savings and tithe)

Debt is not an option. For example, if the child knows he needs a new winter coat for the next season, he has several options. He can save money in his "coat" envelope until he can afford one. He can ask you to take him to yard sales or thrift shops to see if he can purchase a new-to-him coat sooner. Or he can ask an older sibling to sell him a winter coat that no longer fits. What is not an option is asking Mom to buy the coat and owe her for it—that would be going into debt.

Step Three. Calculate savings and tithe for the budget. Both the long-term savings and the tithe amounts should equal 10 percent of the total budget. (This helps train the child to think in terms of tithe 10 percent, save 10 percent, and spend the rest as needed—the most basic of budgets.)

To calculate that, total the amounts in all budget categories apart from savings and tithe (see Example A, subtotal). Multiply that subtotal by 12.5 percent (see Example B below), and the result will be 10 percent of your total budget, which is the amount for savings and the amount for tithe. (I can't explain why it works, but over the years I noticed a pattern. It works.)

EXAMPLE B:	*Figure Savings and Tithe*
Subtotal	$60.00
	x .125
	$ 7.50 each for savings and tithe

Assign that amount to both long-term savings and tithe. The budget is now complete.

EXAMPLE C:	*Total Monthly Budget*
Coat	$5.00
Clothing	$20.00
Shoes	$7.50
Haircut	$7.50
Books	$2.00
Sports	$10.00
Personal	$8.00
Long-term Savings	$7.50
Tithe	$7.50
Total	$75.00

Step Four. Figure what part of the budget is the child's responsibility. See Appendix D for a chart that shows the percent of the budget the child must earn and his hourly wage, given his age. (Feel free to revise the chart to fit your family.) Multiply the child's total monthly budget by the percent you expect him to earn. For example, at age nine, the child is responsible for 10 percent of his budget. A $75 budget times .10 = $7.50. So the child has to earn $7.50 monthly.

Step Five. Translate the child's budget amount into hours of work time per month. To earn that amount, you offer the child an hourly wage that corresponds to his age (see chart in Appendix D). Divide the total he must earn by his hourly wage. That equals the number of hours of paid work-time you expect from the child each month.

Continuing the same example, at age nine the child is paid $1.50 per hour of work time. Divide the $7.50 he has to earn monthly by his hourly wage of $1.50. $7.50 divided by

$1.50 is 5. He owes you five hours of work time per month for the next six months.

Step Six. The child records his work time on a calendar. You give your child a calendar. On the days he works, he should record the hours he worked and what tasks he did. Periodic reminders are recommended. It is much too difficult for either of you to keep track by memory.

You have now established the budget. You have agreed to the amounts per category of the child's budget that you will provide, and the child has agreed to the work time he will provide. Now you are ready to fill in the envelopes and begin budgeting as a joint venture!

Month 1

The fun part for him. Give him an envelope labeled for each category of the budget, except for savings and tithe. Then give him the first month's cash for each category. He is not to mix the money, with the exception that personal allowance may be added to any category if he wants. Provide a colorful zippered bag in which the child can place his envelopes—that's harder to misplace. As soon as you finish, he should place the bag in a safe place.

The money for long-term savings is set aside for the child to take to the bank (or you can write a check for deposit in a money market fund in the child's name). The money for tithe is set aside for the child to take to church the next week (or you can write a check to a charity of the child's choice).

The fun part for you. Provide the child with the calendar to record work time. He will produce this calendar next month to prove he has completed the hours needed for the agreed-upon budget you have just paid. The budget money is paid in advance.

What can he do for work time? He wants to know! Have ideas in mind. Instead of complaining and fighting you about tasks, he will be eager for the budget to work. This contributes to the peace in your home in a variety of ways.

Over the years work time has provided me opportunities to work alongside my children and help them develop many practical skills. They have learned to paint, wallpaper, create and maintain a garden, do yard work, do laundry, clean, and help out with child care. Short-term the children have helped our family; long-term they have gained marketable skills to earn money for college or to cut expenses on their future home.

For the tasks, establish procedures for how to do them and when they should be done. List the procedures on a chart or index card. Do the task with him the first time, explaining any supplies that are needed. Express your gratitude for his help.

Next time supervise the child's work. The more thoroughly you train him, the fewer questions he will have or reminders he will need. Praise his efforts. If you train him well, he will learn how to train younger siblings, further simplifying your work. Watch the magnifying-lens approach: Too much criticism burns.

Month 2 (and Following)

Work time accountability. You begin with the child's work calendar. Has he completed the hours of work? (It is not an option for him not to, unless there are unusual circumstances.)

If he has worked more than the required time, he has two options. He can record it as a credit for the next month's work time. (This is helpful for a child who knows that the next month's sports schedule or other activities will limit his time for work.) Or he can be paid his hourly wage for that additional work time. This extra pay was not part of his budget. Help him figure out 10 percent of it for long-term savings and 10 percent for tithe, to be consistent.

Budget payout. Next you give him cash for the new month, category by category. He places the money in the marked envelopes and puts them away, deposits his savings, and prepares his tithe.

When it is time to shop for clothes or get a haircut, ask your child to bring the pertinent envelope(s) with him. He then has the pleasure and responsibility of paying. This provides many teaching opportunities. Yes, the haircut really costs a dollar more because you have to pay a tip; yes, tax is part of the cost of your new shoes. And your child will have interesting conversations with sales clerks who are amazed that your child budgets.

When six months pass you reexamine the categories with your child. Everything may stay the same, except for the percentage the child provides and the hourly wage for his work time (see the chart in Appendix D). However, there are many reasons for adjusting the categories or the amounts for the next half year. Has he needed as much per month per category as you both originally thought? Has an abundance of hand-me-downs, Christmas or birthday gifts, or a great sale helped him to lower the amount needed in a category temporarily? Maybe a friend is offering haircuts at a discount.

Maybe he has dropped an activity or added one. Possibly grandparents have offered to pay for a sports camp or music lessons, which means altering or dropping a category from the budget for now.

To set up a budget with a child for the first time takes about thirty minutes if you already have the envelopes, cash, and calendar ready. Each month it takes us about fifteen minutes per child to go over work accomplished and pay for the new month.

The difficulties come when I am not prepared to pay them the first of the month, or they have not written down their work time. First solution: I withdraw cash from the bank the week before the first of the month. I also place a reminder card in my stack of bills so I do not forget. Second solution: I remind them after a task is done to record it. They only get credit for what is finished and recorded, so if they forget, they miss out.

It is a challenge to let children make purchases, but with guidance you will be surprised how well they do. Here is one example: One child decided to get an expensive pair of tennis shoes. I was unsure. He noted that he could either buy several cheap pairs over the next six months or one pair of Nikes that would last that long or longer. I let him buy the shoes he wanted. He was right: They did last longer.

The whole concept of having a budget has given me many opportunities to instruct my children in money management and the value of hard work. They think of long-term savings and tithing as parts of their financial life. And they have seen their contribution in work time bless our family in many ways. These principles have given them a head start in adulthood over many of their friends.

THE VALUE OF PLAY

Family life can be serious business. A sense of humor balances the serious work of parenting. In the Hahn family we enjoy punning, as you can tell from my husband's books' subheadings. It is good, clean fun that does not involve put-downs or sarcasm. When we pun at dinner, the laughter helps with digestion.

Plan surprises. Perhaps you could give a child something unexpected for his room. Or you could create a "rainy day" box that only comes out on gloomy days. For a birthday you could write notes to send your child on a treasure hunt. You could gather costume pieces into one closet so your child can find them easily. Perhaps you could select a theme for a dinner or make it extra fancy or extra casual.

We share music as a family. Our children thrive when they have an opportunity to share their musical and artistic accomplishments. Sometimes we have a family concert when relatives visit. At my parents' home over the Christmas holidays, as well as on vacations, our children join their cousins for a talent show. Older cousins inspire younger ones to pick up a particular instrument or to share something they have learned in school that they know the family will appreciate. Older siblings help younger ones in their performances, increasing the shared joy. It is a highlight of our times together every year.

As a family we share literature.[1] We have collections of beloved books. Some we own; some we borrow from the library. Stories fall into different categories. They include fantasy—make-believe but fun. Some are stories about people that could be true but are fictional; others are true biographies. We have enjoyed reading aloud at the end of dinner and before bed.

Sometimes our family chooses a movie or television show to watch together. We have borrowed films from the library or from other families to save rental costs. We have invited families in our history club to join us in watching period films.

Sunday evenings are family game nights. We rotate who gets to choose the game. This limits arguments and guarantees everyone a chance to play his or her favorite game at least once every few weeks. We try to minimize competition and maximize the joy, succeeding to varying degrees.

Special family days can include free concerts in the park, a free day at the local museum, or a picnic to share by a lake. Many families enjoy camping, hiking, and biking together.

Family vacations are not about how much money you spend; they are about maximizing the time together. They are wonderful opportunities to withdraw from ordinary life and spend quality time together to play, to eat, to pray, and to enjoy each other. It takes some effort to build memories, but it is worth it.

The Limited Value of Television

Edith Schaeffer offered this reflection about TV:

> Creative recreation needs a changed mentality to get started: one which does not just shove the children in front of a TV set to keep them quiet but thinks of the challenge as something which will develop into a *person* and at the same time give memories of a childhood to the children which is their own childhood, not just looking into the lives of others on a screen.[2]

We did not own a TV for the first thirteen years of our marriage, and this yielded a number of blessings to our family life and our children's creativity.

Here are some questions to consider. Will you allow your children to watch TV or a movie on school days or school nights? If so, is there a limit? If not, can a child record a show to watch on the weekend? Will you allow a child to watch a show as long as schoolwork is finished? Should your child practice his musical instrument first? Is there a limit to how much time he can watch TV or a film on the weekend? Is there a combined time limit for TV and computer—how much time they can sit in front of a screen watching something? Especially in the summer, do you link TV or computer time to how much time the child reads?

The Value of Good Toys

Choose toys that are worthwhile not only for the money spent and the storage space required but also for the messages they communicate. Little girls develop their nurturing side with cuddly baby dolls. They want to imitate mommy, nursing and caring for the baby. The baby does not have to be anatomically correct for a little girl to change its diapers. But it is nice if it can open its eyes or coo or laugh.

On the other hand, Barbie represents a revolution in the development of dolls. She has an unrealistic body that emphasizes large breasts and no hips. Is it ideal for a little girl to play with a mature-bodied doll who has a boyfriend? Should she think about fashion and makeup as a young girl?

What about guns? Until our oldest son was seven, we determined not to have guns in our home. We held the line in the face of friends who had a range of pistols to star blasters. No matter how shiny the holster or what sounds the gun made, we were not going to encourage violence in our home.

Then we noticed a phenomenon. Duplos became guns. Lincoln Logs became guns. Sticks, forks, and even fingers became guns. Our little boys also came equipped with all of the gun sounds you could imagine. What were we going to do?

We realized that the desire of a little boy to pretend to use a weapon was a God-given impulse to protect and defend good versus evil. Though a weapon could be misused in senseless violence, it did not have to be. A boy's drive to use a weapon could be harnessed for good. So we established certain parameters (not shooting brothers, not pretending to be evil) and bought Michael his first toy rifle. Since then many pistols, daggers, shotguns, and light sabers have found their way into our home, and I think the boys have honored our rules.

If you feel inundated by the number of toys you have on hand, it may be time to weed out toys that break easily or have no educational value. You also might rotate kinds of toys to help the children maintain interest and keep order. Perhaps the children could donate some toys to needy children.

Before acquiring a new toy, ask yourself what value the toy has. Will it last? Does it reinforce creativity for the child and encourage play with others? Grandparents would probably appreciate specific suggestions about the toys you value, since they want to know their money is well spent, strengthening the family.

CONCLUSION

As parents we have the privilege and the responsibility to train our children's hearts, minds, and souls so that they can be all that God has called them to be. In the process, each of us is changed as well. May the Lord show us each day how to build a civilization of love within the walls of our home, so that we can extend that love to others.

CHAPTER SIXTEEN

Trusting God When Parenting Hurts

A ll of us are fruit from the dysfunctional family tree of Adam and Eve. But our baptism grafts us to the family tree of the New Adam, Jesus. How then can we grow in holiness and wholeness as a family? What are the characteristics of that healthy family for which we strive?

Healthy families share core values of faith. They feel a responsibility toward each other, balancing their individual needs and desires with those of the family. They work together, serving each other.

Healthy families communicate with each other. They enjoy conversation, listening as well as sharing. They value conflict resolution over conflict avoidance, even when it is difficult. Parents are approachable about their faults and flaws, which in turn strengthens their children's respect for them.

Healthy families make time for each other. They are loyal, maintaining each other's confidences. They support and enjoy each other. They encourage each other.

We know families who are better at some aspects of this than we are. Instead of comparing our family to another, we can choose mentors who will guide us to improve. Prayerfully we resolve to be better spouses and parents and look for small steps toward honoring that resolution daily.

SHATTERED DREAMS

We have hopes, dreams, and plans for our children. Some of us have already had dreams shattered, hopes dashed, and plans fail. As mothers and fathers we often grieve these losses differently, which can increase our pain.

Some difficulties are health-related. Debilitating illnesses may take huge amounts of money and time away from the rest of the family. Are you in a seemingly endless cycle of doctors' appointments and medicine regimens that are not making your child's pain go away? Are you recovering from a recent miscarriage? Did a child you delivered survive only briefly, leaving your arms aching and your home feeling empty? Is your toddler showing signs of autism?

Some parents have children who suffer from mental health issues—depression, suicidal thoughts, eating disorders, bipolar disorder, and so on. They provide counseling, medication, and even hospitalization. Yet it feels as if there is no end in sight, when their child will feel normal again and life will be normal again.

We receive children with open arms rather than clutching them to ourselves. We are stewards of these precious souls. We are responsible for their care, physically and spiritually, without knowing when we may have to return them to God. Somehow we have to be ready to relinquish a child back to our loving heavenly Father, whose perfect plan may vary greatly from our own.

It seems unnatural when parents bury their child. The Pietà is a vivid picture of a grieving parent relinquishing her son. With open arms Mary holds Jesus' lifeless body, the body she gave him.

When a child dies there are layers of loss—so many "nevers." There are days that seem too normal: How can others act as if today is just another day, when my child is gone? Holidays are extra painful because of the joy that should be there. Parents ache to feel the flesh of their child once more. Odd occurrences can trigger sobbing—a gift not given, a kitchen that stays clean, untouched sports equipment in a corner, an empty bedroom, and silence.

Maybe you are struggling with single parenting, whether your spouse died or abandoned you through divorce. You wonder, how can I be all that my child needs, since I cannot be both Mom and Dad? How can I heal the emotional pain in my children?

Additionally you may ache for a child who is suffering from the unkindness of a sibling, friend, teacher, or fellow student. Perhaps you are trying to help a child cope with failing to make the grade, not being picked for the team or the play, or losing a race.

In the midst of these difficulties, we also sin. Though redeemed, we and our children struggle. "For I do not do the good I want, but the evil I do not want is what I do" (Romans 7:19). How can we as parents "do it right," especially if we feel as if it has already gone horribly wrong? How do we make sense out of our suffering? How can our marriage survive devastating difficulties? Can we pull together so that we do not pull apart? And how do we lift some of the burdens our children carry when the load we carry already seems too heavy for us? No matter how spiritual we are, it is important that we acknowledge our pain and suffering so that Jesus can heal us.

PARENTS IN PAIN

When we as parents are in pain, we struggle with conflicting feelings. We feel guilt, whether or not we have done anything wrong. *How have I failed? Why can't I make this pain go away?* We feel overwhelmed with fear. *What can I change that will not make things worse? How bad will this get if something or someone does not change?* We may have anger toward ourselves, our spouse, our child, or God. *How can this be happening? Why doesn't someone do something?* And we have a deep sense of sadness. *What do I do with the humiliation I feel? How can I move forward?*

In the midst of all of this—the good, the bad, and the ugly—God is at work for good in our lives. Our knowledge about God needs to enter into the core of our aching hearts. He is our place of peace in the storms of life.

Even when all you can do is pray, praying is a lot! Saint Peter urges you, "Cast all your anxieties on him, for he cares about you" (1 Peter 5:7). How do you cast? Like a fisherman who casts his line only to reel it back in? Or as you throw a rock, letting it sink to the depths? The Lord wants you to give him completely the cares that weigh you down.

What if you cannot articulate a prayer? You may have times when the pain is so deep you have to remind yourself to breathe. Even if you can find the words, you may be unsure how to pray. "Likewise the Spirit helps us in our weakness; for we do not know how to pray as we ought, but the Spirit himself intercedes for us with sighs too deep for words" (Romans 8:26). The Spirit prays through us, with us, and for us, even when we cannot formulate a prayer.

OUR HEAVENLY FATHER

Our hearts cry, Lord, where are you in the midst of this suffering? He answers, "I am with you—I am Emmanuel" (which means "God *with* us").

Our heavenly Father has a perspective we lack—an eternal one. He knows all, including how painful a situation is for us and for our children and what it would take to change it. In his infinite love he also knows what is best for us, for our children, and for every person who is or will be affected by our circumstance. In the complex of his knowledge and wisdom, he may say, "Yes, I'll remove it," or, "I'll remove it but not yet," or simply, "No."

Trusting our heavenly Father becomes even more of a challenge when our child is the one who is suffering. We need to allow God to envelope us in his loving arms and give us his strength. He can absorb the sadness and anger of our pain. Throughout the day we pray, "Jesus, I trust in you."

God is all-powerful: He can change any circumstance. If he is not changing something at the moment, there is only one reason why he is not: He loves us too much to change our circumstance. What kind of a father is that, you may wonder?

Our heart may protest, he *cannot* be both all-powerful and all-loving if he *will not* change the situation or person causing me or my child so much pain. Erroneously we lament that, even though God weeps with us, he is not powerful enough to change our circumstances. Or he can change our situation but chooses not to because he *really* does not love us.

Neither explanation describes our heavenly Father, who *is* both all-loving and all-powerful. The witness of our faith proclaims that he holds these two realities in tension, rooted in his fatherly care for us. God alone knows all things. In his divine providence he wills only our good from a heart of love deeper than we can know or understand. *And* he is powerful enough to change our circumstance but will only do so for our greater good. This is the Father's love, which sent his only Son to an agonizing death on the cross so that we might be restored to him.

God is at work for our good in the midst of the depths of suffering we are enduring.

> More than that, we rejoice in our sufferings, knowing that suffering produces endurance, and endurance produces character, and character produces hope, and hope does not disappoint us, because God's love has been poured into our hearts through the Holy Spirit who has been given to us. (Romans 5:3–5)

His Spirit leads us on our journey through suffering to hope. Some of the sting is removed when we thank God in the midst of suffering. "Rejoice always, pray constantly, give thanks in all circumstances; for this is the will of God in Christ Jesus for you" (1 Thessalonians 5:16–18).

A great example of this level of trust is Moses' mother. She delivered Moses when it was politically very difficult for a Hebrew to birth a son. After three months she placed him in a mini-ark in the Nile River, near the place where the Egyptian princess regularly bathed. Think how full of milk her breasts were as she waited to find out what would happen at the riverbank (see Exodus 2:1–10).

Not long after, Moses' sister, Miriam, ran to her mother. The princess had found the baby and needed a Hebrew nurse for him. For Moses' mother it was like getting her son back from the dead! She had entrusted him to God, though she did not know what the outcome would be. God blessed her twofold: with joy at her son's return and with the eventual deliverance of her people, as her son would lead the Israelites out of Egypt into the Promised Land.

You may not know the outcome of your suffering. But you can "know that in everything God works for good with those who love him, who are called according to his purpose" (Romans 8:28). Even when others intend evil, God is still in control. As the patriarch Joseph said to his brothers during their reunion, years after they sold him into slavery, "As for you, you meant evil against me; but God meant it for good" (Genesis 50:20).

God also sends family and friends who will walk with us through the dark valley of suffering. You need not suffer alone. Family and friends can help you as burden bearers and prayer warriors. They will remain with you under the shadow of the cross, just as Mary remained with Jesus. They can hope on your behalf, just as Mary believed Jesus would rise from the dead.

Help is available. Do you belong to a small group Bible study such as the *Life-Nurturing Love* series, in which you can share your concerns and pray together? Can you contact other mothers for prayer (www.mothersprayers.org) or the support group Mothers of Preschool Students (MOPS, www.mops.org)? Ask the Lord to show you a support network that is close at hand.

CASTING OUR CARES ON THE LORD

For the Proverbs 31 woman, "Strength and dignity are her clothing, and she laughs at the time to come" (verse 25). What are our fears for the future in terms of marriage? Children? A move? Finances? Career? Health? We all have valid concerns. What do we do with those concerns? Do we hold on to them, feeding anxiety? Or do we release them to the Lord in prayer?

When I found out I was pregnant after back-to-back miscarriages, I had joy mixed with great fear. Every twinge had me questioning if it was a cramp. I would feel so sick and ask God to help me with my nausea; then I would feel good and panic that the baby had died. Thoughts of possible loss consumed me. I would pray and feel peace momentarily. Then the concerns would crowd my consciousness, and my peace would vanish.

When Father Giles, a good friend, visited our home, I shared my heart and asked for his advice. Gently he said, "Kimberly, your concerns are legitimate—it makes sense you'd fear another miscarriage—but anxiety is sin that you need to confess. 'Have no anxiety about anything, but in everything by prayer and supplication with thanksgiving let your requests be made known to God. And the peace of God, which passes all understanding, will keep your hearts and your minds in Christ Jesus' (Philippians 4:6-7). Let me pray over you."

Then he laid his hand on my head and prayed. I confessed my sin; he pronounced absolution. Almost immediately the gripping anxiety left. I was so grateful that he did not hold back truth, afraid that he might hurt my feelings. He was gentle, reminding me,

> For we have not a high priest who is unable to sympathize with our weaknesses, but one who in every respect has been tempted as we are, yet without sinning. Let us then with confidence draw near to the throne of grace, that we

may receive mercy and find grace to help in time of need.
(Hebrews 4:15–16)

We bring our concerns to the Lord, knowing he hears us, he cares about us, and he will give us the grace we need. Our fears are real, but God's love and power are stronger, for "there is no fear in love, but perfect love casts out fear" (1 John 4:18a). We want him to fill us with his love, so that there is no room for fear.

A couple approached me after I spoke about openness to life. With many tears they shared about the loss of their daughter at birth. They were scared to risk the magnitude of this loss again, yet they felt a conviction about being open. They wondered if *I* thought they should be open. I was grateful they approached me. I would not have wanted them (or anyone) to think that it is my call to make. It is not.

At the same time I was blessed that they shared their hearts with me. They expressed sorrow at their loss and invited me to offer some thoughts. Their suffering had not been wasted: Heaven was richer for the gift of their daughter. Though one child *never* replaces another, a new baby brings healing and comfort. I assured them of my prayers, confident that the Lord would lead them. A year later I received a birth announcement from this couple. Joy had replaced their sense of loss, and they wanted everyone to celebrate with them the gift of new life.

Remember Jesus' call to Peter to walk on water to him (see Matthew 14:22–33)? Jesus could have calmed the waters to help Peter feel less fearful, but he chose not to. When Peter began to sink, Jesus saved him. Like Peter, we must keep our eyes fixed on Jesus. Our trials and difficulties are real, but they are not strong enough to drown us, provided we trust in God.

THE GARDEN OF GETHSEMANE

The Garden of Gethsemane was the place Jesus sweated blood in his agony over the suffering he faced for the redemption of the world. He surrendered his life into his Father's hands. And in that he modeled for us how we must entrust our lives into our heavenly Father's hands precisely at our point of suffering. Though we may feel utterly abandoned, we are never forsaken. He is with us during our times of greatest need.

Visiting the church in the Garden of Gethsemane, I experienced two powerful encounters with our Lord that I want to share.

Since I had successfully delivered our son Jeremiah after back-to-back miscarriages, I thought that that phase of life's loss was over. Late summer 1993, eight weeks prior to our Holy Land pilgrimage, we suffered our third miscarriage. I carried the grief of this fresh loss into my journey.

When we reached the Garden of Gethsemane, it was a bright morning. The church, however, was dim due to the alabaster glass that blocks much of the light. How fitting, I thought, that the church's lighting seemed somber, given what had occurred there.

Praying in this ancient church built over the rock where our Lord sweated blood, I cried out, "Lord, I don't know how to let go of this pain." Gently these words from Isaiah spoke to my heart.

Surely he has borne our griefs
  and carried our sorrows;
yet we esteemed him stricken,
  struck down by God, and afflicted.
But he was wounded for our transgressions,
  he was bruised for our iniquities;
upon him was the chastisement that made us whole,
  and with his stripes we are healed. (Isaiah 53:4–5)

In *that* very place, through Jesus' sufferings, I was healed. All of a sudden I was released from the intensity of the pain. Jesus had not left me alone in my agony, but his agony, in part, was bearing my grief and sorrow. He suffered not only for my sins. I left the church free from the depth of grief that had weighed me down.

Two weeks later I discovered that I was pregnant with Joseph. Set free from the grief of miscarriage, I could share the joy of this new life within.

Five years later we returned to Israel. I was six months pregnant with David, our youngest. We were on the bus, wending our way to the church in the Garden of Gethsemane, as I reflected on my earlier trip there. How much mercy I had experienced through Joseph and now David.

Thinking about Jesus' suffering and my own, I recalled meeting a woman named Teresa the previous summer at a Steubenville conference. Ten years earlier she had suffered a horrific tragedy that she shared with me.

One night she awoke to her children's screaming in terror and pain. She ran to their bedroom, but her estranged husband had barricaded the door. He was killing all three of their children with a hammer, one after the other. She was helpless to intervene. By the time help arrived, her husband had killed the children, set the room on fire, and shot himself. She was unable even to hold her children's lifeless bodies.

For a long time a group of nuns ministered to Teresa as she struggled to survive the pain of her loss. Through them she experienced that "the LORD is near to the brokenhearted, and saves the crushed in spirit" (Psalm 34:18). Then the Lord called her to use her gift in art to create stained glass windows. Each day after a couple of hours before the Blessed Sacrament, she creates stained glass windows, usually of Jesus surrounded by three children.

I was praying for Teresa as our tour bus arrived at the Garden of Gethsemane. We went into the church to pray before Mass. As I knelt, someone tapped me on the shoulder. I turned and saw *Teresa*. She was not a part of our tour; she did not live in Israel. She was visiting Israel for two weeks and had heard that a Franciscan University group would be there.

She began, "I don't know if you remember me." I choked on my tears as I embraced her. "I not only remember you, Teresa, I already prayed for you this morning!"

Throughout Mass I was reminded that if God could meet Teresa's need in the depths of unimaginable suffering, he would certainly meet any suffering I might have to endure. The Lord had placed her on my heart to pray for her, though I had no idea I would see her. He also places my needs on others' hearts, who pray for me as well. He lifts us out of the pit of suffering in his time. "And after you have suffered a little while, the God of all grace, who has called you to his eternal glory in Christ, will himself restore, establish, and strengthen you. To him be the dominion for ever and ever. Amen" (1 Peter 5:10–11).

We commend to Jesus what is incomprehensible. "For my thoughts are not your thoughts, neither are your ways my ways, says the LORD. For as the heavens are higher than the earth, so are my ways higher than your ways and my thoughts than your thoughts" (Isaiah 55:8–9). In the light of eternity, my concerns seem small. Yet these small matters represent God's will in my life, so they are filled with eternal purpose and meaning.

Jesus promises his strength to comfort and fortify us so that we may endure. Even more, he enables us to emerge victorious from our suffering. We choose to trust our heavenly Father to reveal his purposes for our pain and to teach us through it in his time. Sometimes he calms the storm, as Jesus calmed the storm from the boat (see Matthew 8:23–27). Sometimes he comes to us in the midst of the storm and simply tells us to keep our eyes on him (Matthew 14:22–33). We thank him for his love and strength, which sustain us through every storm of life.

THE BEST IS YET TO COME

Through us God is building a civilization of love in our homes—diaper by diaper, day by day! We embrace our beloved through whom we are blessed with motherhood and fatherhood. We thank God that we have the grace we need today to do his will, especially as we mediate that grace to each loved one. Let's pray for each other as we travel this journey together, praising God that he will complete the good work he is doing in and through us.

> Now to him who is able to keep you [and your children] from falling and to present you without blemish before

the presence of his glory with rejoicing, to the only God, our Savior through Jesus Christ our Lord, be glory, majesty, dominion, and authority, before all time and now and for ever. Amen. (Jude 24–25)

APPENDIX A—VIDEO OUTLINES

SESSION ONE: INVITATION TO INTIMACY

I. Review *Life-Nurturing Love* series
   A. *Chosen and Cherished: Biblical Wisdom for Your Marriage* (Proverbs 31:10–12)
   B. *Graced and Gifted: Biblical Wisdom for the Homemaker's Heart* (Proverbs 31:13–17)
   C. *Beloved and Blessed: Biblical Wisdom for Family Life*

II. Life-nurturing love
   A. Interpersonal communion within God (Genesis 1:27)
   B. Invitation to intimacy with God (1 John 4:19)

III. God's design: union and communion
   A. Original solitude and unity (Genesis 2:22–23)
   B. Consecration blessing (Genesis 1:28)
   C. Wedding vow

IV. Invitation to spousal intimacy
   A. Bonding
      1. Vulnerability and indissolubility (Genesis 2:25)
      2. Regardless of intention
      3. Act of covenant renewal
      4. Complementarity (sensual and spiritual)
   B. Babies
      1. Sexuality in service to God
      2. Love incarnate (Psalm 127:3–5)
      3. Lifelong love
      4. Imitation of Christ (Matthew 10:39)
   C. Spousal invitation to intimacy
      1. Date time
      2. Couch time
      3. Snitchin' in the kitchen
      4. Fore-work
      5. Fore-talk
      6. Foreplay

V. Challenges to intimacy
  A. Spiritual
    1. Pleasure permitted? (Genesis 4:1)
    2. Cure for concupiscence (1 Corinthians 7:8–9)
    3. Power play with conjugal duty (1 Corinthians 7:3–5)
    4. Respectful and tender loving care
  B. Physical
    1. Medical issues
    2. Pain
    3. Fatigue
    4. Changing body shape
  C. Interpersonal
    1. Different ways of communicating desires
    2. Different internal clocks
    3. Different needs
    4. Different sexual cycles
    5. Lack of privacy
  D. Psychological
    1. Past traumas
    2. False guilt
    3. Fears
    4. Stress
VI. Defiling the marriage bed
  A. Inappropriate sexual acts
  B. Contraception or sterilization
  C. Pornography
  D. Adultery
VII. Set your heart on your beloved.

SESSION TWO: RESPONSIBLE PARENTHOOD

I. Life-giving love
  A. Family as sanctuary of life
  B. Children are gifts (Psalms 128:3–4)
  C. Natural law

D. Witness of Scripture (Genesis 38:6–10)
E. Witness of Church for two thousand years
F. Lordship of Christ (1 Corinthians 6:19–20; Proverbs 3:5–8)
II. Living sacrifices (Romans 12:1)
   A. By the mercies of God
   B. Your bodies as living sacrifices
   C. Spiritual worship
III. Transformed thinking (Romans 12:2)
   A. Don't be conformed to this world
   B. Transformed by the renewal of your mind
   C. Prove God's will
IV. Results of poor teaching
   A. Misinformed
   B. Frustrated
   C. Confused
   D. Angry and sad
V. *Humanae Vitae:* The mission of responsible parenthood
   A. Power of our fertility
   B. Fragility of our fertility
   C. Generosity of heart
      1. Generosity of Jesus
      2. Imagine the difference …
      3. Generosity to God
   D. Natural Family Planning
      1. God's design
      2. Not the rhythm method
      3. Not the norm of married life
      4. Caution about "planning"
      5. Serious reasons to avoid pregnancy
      6. Tender love
VI. Consequences of contraception
   A. Child is devalued
   B. Teen pregnancies

VII. Train our hearts in truth
    A. Value of sacrificial love (John 15:13)
    B. Value of suffering (Colossians 1:24)
    C. Hope for the future (Romans 8:16–17)
        1. After miscarriage
        2. Infertility
VII. Fundamental conflict of mind-sets:
    The world says   God says
IX. What does it take to live this vision?
    A. Faith
        1. James 4:13–16
        2. Hebrews 4:16
        3. Philippians 4:19
    B. Hope
        1. Romans 8:28
        2. Philippians 4:13
    C. Sacrificial love (Galatians 2:20)
    D. The body of Christ reflects God's love in practical ways
        1. Galatians 6:2
        2. Titus 2:3–5
X. Embrace God's beautiful design for marriage
    A. Respect the sanctity of marriage
    B. Respect the sanctity of life
    C. Deepen understanding of the truth of marital sexuality
    D. Embrace a new beginning (John 8:31–32)

SESSION THREE: FACING THE FUTURE

I. Home by choice
    A. Pressure to work outside the home
    B. Making a difference in your home
II. Home-centered contribution (Proverbs 31:18)
    A. Management of time, talents, and resources
    B. The taste of success
    C. Watchfulness (Luke 12:35–40)
    D. Works with skill (Proverbs 31:19)

III. Household needs come first (Proverbs 31:21)
- A. Prepared for unknown
- B. Meets needs of household
- C. Provides for her needs (Proverbs 31:22)
- D. Clothing for the bride of Christ (Revelations 19:7–8)
- E. Home business (Proverbs 31:24)

IV. Ministry of Presence
- A. Nursing
  1. Bonding
  2. Protection
  3. Nutrition
  4. Benefits to baby
  5. Benefits to mom
- B. Mediating God's grace (Psalm 22:9; Isaiah 66:10–13)
  1. Contributes to family's well-being
  2. Economics of a stay-at-home mom (Psalm 127:1)

V. Teamwork for financial future
- A. Budget
  1. Plan for success (Luke 14:28–30)
  2. Pray before you spend
  3. Self-control (Luke 12:15)
  4. Long-term (Proverbs 13:11)
- B. Tithing (Malachi 3:8, 10)
- C. Stewardship of possessions (Hebrews 13:5)
- D. Avoid debt (Proverbs 11:14)

VI. Facing our fears (Proverbs 31:25)
  1. Difference between concerns and anxiety (Hebrews 4:15–16)
  2. Perfect love casts out fear (1 John 4:18)
  3. Strength and dignity (Proverbs 31:25; Philippians 4:11–12)
  4. She laughs at the time to come (Malachi 3:6; Hebrews 13:8)

VII. Mary's motherhood
- A. Consents to the unknown (Luke 1:26–38)
- B. Consents to serve (Luke 1:39–56; Mark 10:45)

C. Consents to follow her husband's leadership (Matthew 2:13–15)

D. Consents to live a hidden life (Luke 2:19, 34–35, 51–52)

E. Consents to love at a distance (Luke 11:27–28)

F. Consents to suffer alongside her son (John 19:25–27)

G. Consents to continue to serve (Revelation 12:17)

SESSION FOUR: THE PERFECT PARENT

I. A good reputation (Proverbs 31:23)

    A. Criteria for bishop: husband; father of obedient children (1 Timothy 3:4-5)

    B. "Known in the gates" (Ruth 4:11)

    C. "Sits among elders"

II. The perfect parent: God the Father

    A. Delights in us (Proverbs 3:12)

    B. Is present to us—Immanuel

    C. Governs us with wisdom (Proverbs 4:10–11)

    D. Lavishes us with grace (Matthew 7:9–11)

    E. Is slow to anger and kind (Nehemiah 9:17)

    F. Expects but does not force obedience

    G. Reproves us

    H. Disciplines us because we are his children (Hebrews 12:5–11)

    I. Even God has rebellious children (Isaiah 1:2)

    J. Father sacrifices to restore us to himself

III. The privilege of parenting

    A. Vowed publicly to receive children

    B. We have been chosen to care for their needs and their education

    C. We are under authority: firmly parent with S.O.F.T. hearts

        • S =

        • O =

        • F =

        • T =

IV. Imitate God's fatherly care
   A. Delight in each child
   B. Become a student of each child
      1. Personality: Myers/Briggs Personality Inventory
      2. Temperament: Father Conrad Hock's article
      3. Love language: *Five Love Languages for Children* by Gary Chapman
   C. Discipline your child (Proverbs 22:6)
      1. Every interaction is an act of formation
      2. Proverbs 19:18
      3. Never too late to adjust
V. Models of Parenting
   1. Authoritarian
   2. Permissive (Proverbs 29:15)
   3. Neglectful
   4. Authoritative
   5. Parental control to self-control model
VI. Necessity of fathers
   A. New covenant promise (Malachi 4:5–6)
   B. Uses God's Word well (Proverbs 30:5)
   C. What happens when fathers fail?
   D. Strength of a father
      1. Rely on the Lord (Sirach 5:2)
      2. Don't be a lion (Sirach 4:30)
      3. Strength *for* them
   E. Moms' support for husbands
   F. Anger in discipline
      1. Self-control is important (Proverbs 14:17; 25:28)
      2. Fathers, don't provoke children (Colossians 3:20, 21; Ephesians 6:4)
      3. Applies to moms too
VII. Five keys to setting boundaries with your child
   A. Lead with love
   B. Differentiate between moral absolutes and wise counsel

C. C.L.E.A.R. guidelines
- C
- L
- E
- A
- R

D. Record rules to assist memory

E. Try to catch them doing ... right!

VIII. Seven Methods of Correction

    A. Communication (Sirach 11:7–8)

    B. Natural consequences (Wisdom 11:15–16)

    C. Logical consequences (2 Thessalonians 3:10)

    D. Reinforcement

    E. Time out

    F. Spanking (Proverbs 13:24)

    G. Grounding

    H. Caution on sensitivity to love languages

IX. Closed spirits

    A. A child's closed spirit
1. We want to bend will without breaking spirit
2. Sometimes we wound our child's spirit (Proverbs 13:12)
3. Children withdraw, withhold affection, become rebellious

    B. Our response
1. Pray to make it right
2. Talk with your child with respect—be vulnerable
3. Ask forgiveness for any wrongdoing
4. Be tenderhearted: Make deposits in emotional bank

    C. Closed spirit toward your child
1. Acknowledge difficulty to God; ask for his heart for your child
2. Ponder the gift this child has been: birth, childhood
3. Ask God to help you see the child's true need right now

    4. Thank God for that child: God wants to do something in you!

    5. Identify root cause of difficulty: is the child like you? unlike you?

    6. Imagine child ten years from now

IX. If you are a parent …

  A. You have the authority to speak the truth in love

  B. You have the love to overcome your fears

  C. You have the obligation to continue the job you began until you are done

SESSION FIVE: MAKING A HOME FOR THE WORD

I. Introduction (Proverbs 31:26)

  A. To parent is to teach

  B. Qualifications (*CCC*, 2252)

  C. Words and deeds

    1. How was Jesus taught the faith? (Psalms 31:5)

    2. How did Jesus catechize?

    3. Our family as the domestic church (*CCC*, 1666)

  D. Great Commission (Matthew 28:19–20)

II. Build a home for the Word (Proverbs 12:7)

  A. By wisdom (Proverbs 24:3–4)

  B. Foundation: Jesus and the apostles (Ephesians 2:19–22)

  C. Walls: building materials of our good works (1 Corinthians 3:12–13)

  D. Roof: covering by our consecration (Proverbs 14:26; John 17:19)

  E. Door: open to our Lord (Revelation 3:20)

III. Deuteronomy 6:4–7: focus on heart and soul

  A. Our relationship with God

  B. Our children: educating the whole person to love God

  C. How are we to teach? When? Where?

  D. Teachable moments

IV.   2 Timothy 3:14–17
    A. Background—received from childhood a love for Scripture
    B. Role of the Holy Spirit
      1. Holy Spirit inspired sacred Scripture
      2. Holy Spirit preserves infallible interpretation of sacred Scripture
    C. Examine the Scriptures
      1. Teaching—understand the faith
      2. Reproof—identify doctrinal error
      3. Correction—behavior brought to a standard
      4. Training in righteousness—how to grow in holiness (Psalm 119:9, 11)
      5. Equipped for every good work (Hebrews 4:12)
V.   Study the Word carefully (Ephesians 6:17)
    A. Handle "sword" well (2 Timothy 2:15)
    B. Memorize—"sword" drills (Philippians 1:21)
VI.   Develop a domestic liturgy: sharing the Word with our family
    A. Children are spiritually sensitive
    B. A rhythm of prayer (*CCC*, 2685)
      1. Morning prayer
      2. Throughout the day
      3. Evening prayers
    C. Mass
      1. Sunday (Hebrews 10:24–25)
      2. Weekday Masses
      3. Visits to the Blessed Sacrament
    D. The liturgical calendar
      1. Advent and Christmas; Lent and Easter
      2. Sacrament preparation
      3. Religious art
VII. Character formation: the tongue
    A. Words reveal the heart (Matthew 12:34b–37)
    B. Words are powerful (James 3:3–6a, 9–10: bridle, rudder, fire)
    C. Blessing and curse—use of the tongue—see Appendix F
VIII. It's never too late to live the faith well as a family

SESSION SIX: TO SCULPT A LIFE — PARENTING OVER THE LONG HAUL

I.   Creating a civilization of love (Proverbs 31:26)

II. Educating the whole person (Deuteronomy 6:4–6)
- Goal of truly Christian education (1 Corinthians 8:1)

III. Academic skills

    A. Principle of subsidiarity (*Catholic Education: Homeward Bound* by Kimberly Hahn and Mary Hasson)

    B. Instill values—yours!

IV. Socialization

    A. Difficulties

    B. Purpose (Proverbs 13:20)

    C. Home is the natural environment for socialization

    D. Foster relationships between siblings to last a lifetime (Proverbs 3:27)

    E. Work through conflicts (Proverbs 18:19)

    F. Stay involved no matter how your child is educated

V. Train in practical life skills

    A. Contribution to family and sense of self-worth

    B. Value of chores (Colossians 3:23–24)

    C. Train in money management with kids' budgets

        1. Kids' budgets (*Money Matters for Parents and Their Kids* by Ron and Judy Blue)

        2. Personal chores: unpaid work

        3. Establish categories: no debt; cash in envelopes

        4. Look at monthly budget; check chart in Appendix D for percentage to earn and hourly wage

        5. Work time: See Appendix D

        6. Month 2: child proves work time; Mom pays for extra work and provides envelopes

        7. Chores: what do they need from us to succeed?
- Establish specific procedures, provide supplies, supervise, praise.

    D. Practical skills: painting, wallpapering, gardening, yard work …

E.   Apprenticeships; help with family business

F.   Sex education—need-to-know basis *(Maidenhood Seminar)*

VI.   Family policies on media—

   A.   C.L.E.A.R. boundaries

   B.   Computer and the Internet

   C.   TV

VII.   Ways to encourage family fun—balance with being serious!

   A.   Sense of humor

   B.   Be creative

   C.   Music shared

   D.   Literature shared

   E.   Toys

   F.   Family movie night or game night

   G.   Planned family events—hospitality, vacations

VIII.   Parents in pain

   A.   Crises

   B.   Our struggles

   C.   Trusting our heavenly Father (1 Peter 5:7)

      1.   Romans 8:26

      2.   Romans 5:3–5

      3.   Moses' mother (see Exodus 2:1–10)

   D.   Support for mothers: like-minded family and friends; Life-Nurturing Love groups; Mothers' Prayers; MOPS

   E.   The Garden of Gethsemane, where Jesus had to trust his Father (Isaiah 55:8–9)

IX.   The best is yet to come, as God builds a civilization of love in our homes (Jude 24–25)

Appendix B

Questions for an Intergenerational Women's Study

Session One
1. What messages do we get from our culture that conflict with biblical truth about sexuality?
2. What expectations did you bring to marriage on issues related to marital intimacy?
3. Is the lack of privacy, energy, or time impairing your sexual intimacy? How can you address these issues?
4. In what ways can you and your spouse create a more playful or romantic spirit in the bedroom?
5. Are you and your spouse able to find time to nurture the core relationship of the family, so that your children feel secure in your love for each other?
6. For personal private reflection: Am I meeting my husband's needs? Is he meeting mine? Can we discuss this?

Session Two
1. How do Jesus' words, "You will know the truth and the truth will make you free" (John 8:32) apply in the area of Christian sexuality?
2. Were there specific materials about the Church's teaching on sex that helped you and your husband prepare for marriage?
3. When talking with someone considering marriage, what do you think is the most important point to emphasize regarding Church teaching about marriage?
4. Are you familiar with Natural Family Planning? Do you understand how NFP is different from contraception?
5. Do you have support in your extended family for following the Church's teaching on openness to life? If not, how do you handle dissenting comments?
6. If you have lost a child in miscarriage or stillbirth, what most

helped you with your loss? Was there anything you wish someone had said or done?

7. If you have struggled with infertility—temporary or permanent
—what has helped? Is there anything you wish others would
say or do?

SESSION THREE

1. How were finances handled in your home when you were a
child? Budgets or not? Savings or living on the edge, not paying
bills? Paying bills in full or paying minimums on credit cards?
2. Were there conflicts about money in your family, and if so, what
was the source of that conflict?
3. What is your most important financial goal?
4. Are you financially leaving your parents and cleaving to your
spouse? Is it difficult to accept financial help from parents without feeling as if there are strings attached?
5. Is it possible to live on a budget? Is it possible to live without
credit cards?
6. What has been your biggest financial adjustment since getting
married?
7. What do you think about working from home?
8. Is it possible today for moms to be home with their young children? What are the advantages, and what are the challenges?
9. What is the biggest sacrifice for a stay-at-home mom?
10. Did you grow up imagining yourself at home with your
children?
11. What would you say to a friend whose husband is not support-
ive of her being at home when they have children?
12. How is Mary a model for you as a mother?

SESSION FOUR

For each child:

1. List three words that best describe this child
2. What is the most delightful thing about my child?
3. List two strengths of this child and his or her major weakness

4. What is my child's temperament? Personality? Love language?
5. What is this child's primary need right now?
6. Is there one area of our relationship on which I can focus my energy?

General questions:
1. What method of discipline do you find most effective?
2. If you have a spread of ages, what helps you vary discipline so that you don't treat a teen like a toddler (especially when he may act like one)?
3. Is there one resource that has helped you more than others in the area of discipline?
4. How is anger handled in your home?
5. Is it possible to be a mediator in the home without positioning yourself between your spouse and your child? If your spouse is provoking a child to anger, how can you help him understand without undermining his authority?
6. What is your parenting style: authoritarian, permissive, neglectful, authoritative? What do you want it to be?
7. How do you differentiate between childishness and sinful behavior?
8. Why is it more important to be strict when children are young and then allow more freedoms as they get older?
9. Regarding bedtimes, schedules, pop culture, homework, dress code, computer use, time with friends, and TV watching—what rules did you have growing up or have now you established? How do you keep track so that you are consistent?

SESSION FIVE
1. In what way are parents catechists?
2. How can you get to know the faith better so that you can teach your children?
3. How can you "let the word of Christ dwell in you richly" (Colossians 3:16)?
4. What is the most helpful resource you have found to share God's

Word with your children?

5. When is the best time of day for your family to pray?

6. How can your words contribute to the well-being of your spouse and children?

7. How can you help your children be more loving toward each other with the things they say? Can the verses read today help you point your children to the standard you expect of them, a standard that applies to you as well?

SESSION SIX

1. How can we guide our children to be more loving toward each other?

2. How does home life prepare each of us to be a better brother or sister in Christ to those outside our family?

3. How do we guide our children to be good friends and to choose good friends?

4. What does it mean to "keep short accounts" in terms of conflict resolution? How does that apply to our children with their siblings?

5. How do you approach chores in your family?

6. How have you guided your children in managing money?

7. Have you used budgets with your children?

8. Have you established family policies for media? What helps you and your husband to present a united front?

9. What does your family do for fun?

10. When you as a parent have been in pain—for your child or because of your child—what has most helped you to cope?

11. How can women support one another as we face the many challenges involved in the vocation of marriage and family life?

APPENDIX C

FAMILY BUDGET ITEMS

Monthly Paid Other	Annual Amount	Paid Monthly	Paid Other Than Monthly
HOUSING			
Mortgage or rent			
Rental or homeowners' insurance			
Property taxes			
Electricity			
Natural gas			
Water			
Sanitation			
Telephone			
Cell phone(s)			
Internet			
Cleaning: labor			
Supplies for cleaning			
Repairs/maintenance			
Home improvements			
Home furnishings			
TOTAL HOUSING			
FOOD			
CLOTHING			
TRANSPORTATION			
Insurance			
License plate(s)			
Gas and oil			
Maintenance/repairs			
Parking			
Tolls			
Bus or train			

Savings toward the next car TOTAL TRANSPORTATION			
ENTERTAINMENT/RECREATION *Dates* *Magazines/newspapers/cable* *Vacation* *Clubs and activities* TOTAL ENTERTAINMENT			
MEDICAL EXPENSES *Insurance* *Copays* *Dentists* *Prescriptions* *Other* TOTAL MEDICAL			
LIFE INSURANCE			
CHILDREN *Allowances* *Books* *College/tuition* *Music lessons* *Sports* *Other* TOTAL CHILDREN			
GIFTS *Christmas* *Birthdays* *Anniversaries* *Graduations* *Sacraments* *Other* TOTAL GIFTS			

MISCELLANEOUS
  Toiletries
  Husband: lunches, and
    other expenses
  Wife: miscellaneous
  Dry cleaning
  Animals (licenses, food, vet)
  Beauty/barber
  Other
TOTAL MISCELLANEOUS			

TOTAL LIVING EXPENSES			

Appendix D

Kids' Budgets

- Choose the budget categories; give your child an envelope for each.
- Determine the budget per category.
- Total the working budget.
- Multiply the working budget by .125 for tithe and savings.
- Add in tithe and savings for the total budget.
- For the child's age, what percent of the budget does he owe?
- Multiply his total budget by the percent he owes.

Age	Percent of Budget child pays	Hourly Wage
8	5%	1.00
8-1/2	5%	1.25
9	10%	1.50
9-1/2	15%	1.75
10	20%	2.00
10-1/2	25%	2.50
11	30%	3.00
11-1/2	35%	3.50
12	40%	4.00
12-1/2	45%	4.50
13	50%	5.00
13-1/2	55%	5.25
14	60%	5.50
14-1/2	65%	5.75
15	70%	6.00
15-1/2	75%	6.25
16	80%	6.50
16-1/2	85%	6.75
17	90%	7.00
17-1/2	95%	7.25
18	100%	7.50

- For the child's age, what is his hourly wage?
- Divide total he owes by his hourly wage for hours of work time he owes.

Month 1:
- Pay the budget with cash for each envelope.
- Give him a colorful zippered bag in which to store the envelopes.
- Give him a calendar to record work time.

Month 2 and following:
- Settle up work time from the month just finished using the calendar.
- Decide what to do with additional work time if there is any.
- Provide cash for each envelope for this month.

After six months reexamine the budget:
- Add or subtract categories.
- Adjust amounts up or down as needed. Then proceed as usual.

APPENDIX E

STEWARDSHIP OF THE HOME

WARRANTY INFORMATION
1. Keep a record of warranties handy so you can use them easily.
2. If your receipt is part of your warranty, do not file it with tax paperwork that could be thrown away.
3. File the warranties in a pocket folder behind this sheet.
4. If you sell your home, you can provide warranties to the buyer.

Date of warranty (from when to when) _____
Serial number of product _____
Date of purchase _____
Maintenance checkups? When? _____
_____

DECORATING DETAILS

1. Record details: date decorated, what paint you used where, and the number of wallpaper or border rolls needed (so you never measure that room again).
2. Designate a place to put paint (good for three years) to use later for touch-ups. Write with an indelible marker on the can when and where that paint was used.
3. Record warranty information about the carpet or flooring.

Date _____

Type of paint: name, number, company _____

Rolls of wallpaper used _____

Carpet: details for company warranty _____

_____

MAJOR HOME IMPROVEMENTS

1. Maintain good records so that if you sell your home, you can prove how much you have actually paid in home improvements.
2. Note when minor maintenance checks should occur to avert major difficulties.
3. Note major improvements to factor into next year's budget, so you are not blindsided by unexpected large bills.

Date _____

Improvement _____

Company purchased from _____

Warranty details _____

Maintenance or repair contract _____

_____

Appendix F

The Power of the Tongue

I. Sins of the tongue
    A. Many words (Proverbs 10:19)
    B. Rash words (Proverbs 12:18, 19)
    C. Lies (Proverbs 12:22)
    D. Men stir up strife with false teaching (Titus 1:10, 11)
    E. Women spread gossip (1 Timothy 5:13)
    F. Slander (Proverbs 10:18)
II. Choices we can make
    A. Imitate God's life-giving speech (Colossians 3:7–10)
    B. Do not gossip (Proverbs 20:19)
    C. Share truth, not folly (Proverbs 15:2, 4)
    D. Quell a quarrel (Proverbs 26:20)
    E. Use gracious speech (Colossians 4:6)
    F. Think before you speak (Proverbs 15:28)
    G. Restrain speech (Proverbs 17:27)
    H. Edify others (Ephesians 4:29, 31–32)
    I. Bring health to others (Proverbs 16:23–24; 25:25)
    J. Control the tongue (Psalms 141:3)
    K. Defend the faith (1 Peter 3:14, 15)

RECOMMENDED RESOURCES

BOOKS

Aquilina, Mike. *Love in the Little Things: Tales of Family Life.* Cincinnati: Servant, 2007.

Bennett, Art and Laraine. *The Temperament God Gave You: The Classic Key to Knowing Yourself, Getting Along with Others, and Growing Closer to the Lord.* Manchester, N.H.: Sophia, 2005.

Blue, Ron and Judy. *Money Matters for Parents and Their Kids.* Nashville: Oliver-Nelson, 1988; republished and retitled *Raising Money-Smart Kids.* Nashville: Nelson, 1992.

Bradley, Robert. *Husband-Coached Childbirth.* New York: Harper & Row, 1965.

Catechism of the Catholic Church, 2nd ed. Vatican City: Libreria Editrice Vaticana, 1997.

Chapman, Gary. *The Five Love Languages: How to Express Heartfelt Commitment to Your Mate.* Chicago: Northfield, 1995.

_____ and Ross Campbell. *The Five Love Languages of Children.* Chicago: Northfield, 1997.

Dobson, James. *The New Dare to Discipline.* Wheaton, Ill.: Tyndale House, 1992.

_____. *The Strong-Willed Child.* Wheaton, Ill.: Tyndale House, 1985.

Elliot, Elisabeth. *The Shaping of a Christian Family—How My Parents Nurtured My Faith.* Grand Rapids: Revell, 1992.

Escrivá, Josemaría. *The Way.* New York: Random House, 2006.

Hahn, Kimberly. *Chosen and Cherished: Biblical Wisdom for Your Marriage.* Cincinnati: Servant, 2007.

_____. *Graced and Gifted: Biblical Wisdom for the Homemaker's Heart.* Cincinnati: Servant, 2008.

_____. *Life-Giving Love: Embracing God's Beautiful Design for Marriage.* Cincinnati: Servant, 2001.

_____ and Mary Hasson. *Catholic Education: Homeward Bound: A Useful Guide to Catholic Home Schooling.* San Francisco: Ignatius, 1996.

Hahn, Scott. *Signs of Life: 40 Catholic Customs and Their Biblical Roots.* New York: Doubleday, 2009.

_____ and Leon J. Suprenant, eds. *Catholic for a Reason II: Scripture and the Mystery of the Mother of God.* Steubenville, Ohio: Emmaus Road, 2000.

_____ and Regis J. Flaherty, eds. *Catholic for a Reason IV: Scripture and the Mystery of Marriage and Family Life.* Steubenville, Ohio: Emmaus Road, 2007.

John Paul II. *Evangelium Vitae* [The Gospel of Life]. Encyclical on the Value and Inviolability of Human Life, March 25, 1995. www.vatican.va.

_____. *Gratissimam sane.* Letter to Families. February 2, 1994. www.vatican.va.

_____. *Love and Responsibility.* H.T. Willetts, trans. San Francisco: Ignatius, 1993.

Kippley, John F. *Sex and the Marriage Covenant: A Basis for Morality.* Cincinnati: Couple to Couple League, 1991.

Kippley, Sheila K. and John F. *The Art of Natural Family Planning,* 4th ed. Cincinnati: Couple to Couple League, 1996.

Kippley, Sheila K. *Breastfeeding and Catholic Motherhood: God's Plan for You and Your Baby.* Manchester, N.H.: Sophia Institute Press, 2005.

_____. *Breastfeeding and Natural Child Spacing: The Ecology of Natural Mothering.* Cincinnati: Couple to Couple League, 1999.

La Leche League. *The Womanly Art of Breastfeeding.* New York: Plume, 1991.

Lenahan, Phil. *7 Steps to Becoming Financially Free: A Catholic Guide to Managing Your Money.* Huntington, Ind.: Our Sunday Visitor, 2006.

Martin, Michaelann, Carol Puccio, and Zöe Romanowski. *The Catholic Parent Book of Feasts: Celebrating the Church Year With Your Family.* Huntington, Ind.: Our Sunday Visitor, 1999.

Matthews, Elizabeth. *Precious Treasure: The Story of Patrick.* Steubenville, Ohio: Emmaus Road, 2002.

McCluskey, Christopher and Rachel. *When Two Become One: Enhancing Sexual Intimacy in Marriage.* Grand Rapids: Revell, 2004.

McCullough, Bonnie Runyan and Susan Walker Monson. *401 Ways to Get Your Kids to Work at Home.* New York: St. Martin's, 1981.

McElhone, James F. *Particular Examen: How to Root Out Hidden Faults.* Notre Dame, Ind.: Ave Maria, 1953.

Orman, Suze. *The Money Book for the Young, Fabulous & Broke.* New York: Riverhead, 2005.

Paul VI. *Humanae Vitae* [Of Human Life]. Encyclical on the Regulation of Birth. July 25, 1968. www.vatican.va.

Pierlot, Holly. *A Mother's Rule of Life: How to Bring Order to Your Home and Peace to Your Soul.* Manchester, N.H.: Sophia, 2004.

Ramsey, Dave. *The Total Money Makeover: A Proven Plan for Financial Fitness.* Nashville: Nelson, 2007.

Russell, William F. *Classics to Read Aloud to Your Children.* New York: Crown, 1984.

Schaeffer, Edith. *The Hidden Art of Homemaking: Creative Ideas for Enriching Everyday Life.* Wheaton, Ill.: Tyndale House, 1971.

Shannon, Marilyn. *Fertility, Cycles and Nutrition.* Cincinnati: Couple to Couple League, 2001. www.nfpandmore.org.

Wilson, Elizabeth. *Books Children Love: A Guide to the Best Children's Literature.* Westchester, Ill.: Crossway, 1987.

Young, Pamela I. and Peggy A. Jones. *Sidetracked Home Executives: From Pigpen to Paradise.* New York: Warner, 2001.

OTHER RESOURCES

Apostolate for Family Consecration sponsors Catholic Familyland (for family retreats and catechesis), 3375 County Road 36, Bloomingdale, OH 43910-9901; (740) 765-5500; www.familyland.org.

Apostolate of Hannah's Tears, http://theapostolateofhannahstears. blogspot.com, for prayer support and practical help for all who suffer infertility (at any stage), difficult pregnancies or the loss of a child.

Billings Ovulation Method Association, USA: resource for Natural Family Planning. P.O. Box 2135, St. Cloud, MN 56302; (651) 699-8139; www.boma-usa.org.

Burkett, Larry. "A Guide to Financial Freedom." www.cbn.com.

Couple to Couple League: resource for Natural Family Planning. P. O. Box 111184, Cincinnati, OH 45211-1184; (513) 471-2000; www.ccli.org. A number of excellent pamphlets are available, including "Tubal Ligation: Some Questions and Answers."

Haven of Hope and Healing, Inc.: pregnancy and infant loss resource. P. O. Box 747, Graham, NC 27253; (336) 227-8306; www.havenofhopeandhealing.org.

Hock, Conrad. "The Four Temperaments." www.angelicum.net.

Kippley, John and Sheila. www.naturalfamilyplanningandmore.org and www.catholicbreastfeeding.org

La Leche League: breast-feeding information and support. www.llli.org.

Mother's Prayers of the Solace Community: thousands of women's prayer groups throughout the world, focusing on prayer for children. www.mothersprayers.org.

National Coalition for the Protection of Children & Families: anti-pornography organization. www.nationalcoalition.org

One More Soul fosters God's plan for love, marriage, and procreation. 1846 N. Main St., Dayton, OH 45405; (800) 307-7685; www.omsoul.com. Resources available: "Marriage: A Communion of Life and Love," a pastoral letter by Bishop Victor Galeone, diocese of Augustine; Steve Patton's CD "Why Contraception Matters: How It Keeps Us From Love and Life"; Chris Kahlenborn and Ann Moell, "What a Woman Should Know About Contraceptives."

Parenting With Christ, a Catholic faith-based program instilling hope for families of the new millennium. (877) 792-4747. www.parentingwithchrist.com.

Pope Paul VI Institute offers diagnosis and treatment for reproductive disorders. 6901 Mercy Rd., Omaha, NE 68106; (402) 390-6600; www.popepaulvi.com.

Postpartum depression resources: postpartum.net and ppdhope.com.

Pregnancy and Infant Loss Center, Inc., 1521 E. Wayzata Blvd., Suite 30, Wayzata, MN 55391-1939; (952) 473-9372.

Project Rachel operates as a network of professional counselors and priests trained to provide one-on-one spiritual and psychological care for people suffering because of an abortion. National Office of Post Abortion Reconciliation and Healing, (800) 5WE-CARE, www.hopeafterabortion.com.

Rachel's Vineyard Ministries offers weekend retreats and other healing resources for those who have been involved in abortion. 808 N. Henderson Road, 2nd Floor, King of Prussia, PA 19406; (610) 354-0555. www.rachelsvineyard.com.

Retrouvaille, a ministry for couples with serious marital difficulties. (800) 470-2230. www.retrouvaille.org.

St. Joseph's Covenant Keepers, a ministry for families. Family Life Center, 2130 Wade Hampton Blvd., Greenville, SC 29615; (864) 268-6730. www.dads.org.

St. Paul Center for Biblical Theology: resources for parish-based and online Bible studies for laypeople. 2228 Sunset Blvd., Suite 2A, Steubenville, OH 43952; (740) 264-9535; www.salvation history.com.

Sexaholics Anonymous International Central Office, P. O. Box 3565, Brentwood, TN 37024; (615) 370-6062 or (866) 424-8777; saico@sa.org. sexaholics.org

Share Pregnancy and Infant Loss Support, Inc. The Share Office, 402 Jackson St., St. Charles, MO 63301; (636) 947-6164; (800) 821-6819. www.nationalshare.org.

Society of St. Gianna Beretta Molla promotes holiness in the family and the sanctity of human life. P.O. Box 2946, Warminster, PA 18974; (215) 333-0145. www.saintgianna.org.

TORCH (Traditions of Roman Catholic Homes) offers homeschooling support through forty-two chapters in sixteen states. www.torchhomeschooling.org.

VIDEO SERIES

Hahn, Kimberly. *Life-Nurturing Love* series in four installments of six
Bible studies each. First set is *Chosen and Cherished: Biblical
Wisdom for Your Marriage.* Second set is *Graced and Gifted:
Biblical Wisdom for the Homemaker's Heart.* Third set is *Beloved
and Blessed: Biblical Wisdom for Family Life* (Cincinnati: Servant,
2007–2010).

NOTES

PART ONE: THE HEART OF HER HUSBAND TRUSTS IN HER
CHAPTER ONE: INVITATION TO INTIMACY

1. See Pope Benedict XVI, *Deus Caritas Est,* Encyclical on Christian Love, December 25, 2005, no. 10, www.vatican.va.
2. Pope John Paul II, Apostolic Letter *On the Dignity and Vocation of Women,* August 15, 1988, no. 7, www.priestsforlife.org.
3. *Deus Caritas Est,* no. 11.
4. *On the Dignity and Vocation of Women,* no. 18.
5. Pope Paul VI, *Humanae Vitae,* Encyclical on the Regulation of Birth, July 25, 1968, no. 8, www.vatican.va.
6. Pope Pius XI, *Casti Connubii,* Encyclical on Christian Marriage, December 31, 1930, no. 23, www.vatican.va.
7. Pope John Paul II, *Letter to Families,* February 2, 1994, no. 11, www.vatican.va.
8. *On the Dignity and Vocation of Women,* no. 29.
9. *Deus Caritas Est,* no. 4.
10. *Deus Caritas Est,* no. 5.
11. Christopher and Rachel McCluskey, *When Two Become One: Enhancing Sexual Intimacy in Marriage* (Grand Rapids: Revell, 2004), figure 5.2.

CHAPTER TWO: CHALLENGES TO INTIMACY

1. *Humanae Vitae,* no. 11.
2. *Letter to Families,* no. 13.
3. Pope Paul VI Institute, 6901 Mercy Rd., Omaha, NE 68106; (402) 390-6600, www.popepaulvi.com.
4. Karol Wojtyla (Pope John Paul II), *Love and Responsibility,* H.T. Willetts, trans. (New York: Farrar, Straus, Giroux, 1982), p. 273.
5. Wojtyla, p. 179, emphasis added.
6. Rachel's Vineyard Ministries offers weekend retreats and other healing resources for those who have been involved in abortion. 808 N. Henderson Road, 2nd Floor, King of Prussia, PA 19406, (610) 354-0555, www.rachelsvineyard.com.

7. National Coalition for the Protection of Children & Families, www.nationalcoalition.org; Sexaholics Anonymous International Central Office, P. O. Box 3565, Brentwood, TN 37024, (615) 370-6062 or (866) 424-8777, saico@sa.org., www.sexaholics.org

8. Retrouvaille, www.retrouvaille.org, (800) 470-2230.

PART TWO: HER CHILDREN RISE UP AND CALL HER BLESSED

CHAPTER THREE: FAMILY AS THE SANCTUARY OF LIFE

1. Pope Benedict XVI, Commentary on Psalm 126 (127), September 1, 2005, no. 4, italics mine.

2. Vatican II, *Gaudium et Spes,* Pastoral Constitution on the Church in the Modern World, no. 50, www.vatican.va.

3. *On the Dignity and Vocation of Women,* no. 30.

4. *On the Dignity and Vocation of Women,* no. 18.

5. *On the Dignity and Vocation of Women,* no. 18.

6. *Letter to Families,* no. 16.

7. *Letter to Families,* no. 11.

8. Janet Smith, "Natural Law and Sexual Ethics," pp. 9, 10, www.goodmorals.org.

9. Ernee Lawagan, "The Birth of Birth Control," www.globalpinoy.com.

10. *Casti Connubii,* no. 56.

11. Pope John Paul II, *Evangelium Vitae* [The Gospel of Life], Encyclical on the Value and Inviolability of Human Life, March 25, 1995, no. 23, www.vatican.va.

CHAPTER FOUR: THE MISSION OF RESPONSIBLE PARENTHOOD

1. *Humanae Vitae,* no. 10.

2. Wojtyla, p. 230.

3. Pope John Paul II, quoting *Humanae Vitae,* no. 10, in his general audience of August 1, 1984, "Pope John Paul II on Marriage: Responsible Parenthood," no. 5, www.catholic-pages.com.

4. *Humanae Vitae,* introduction.

5. "Natural Family Planning," www.bygpub.com.

6. *Evangelium Vitae,* no. 97.

CHAPTER FIVE: ANSWERING THE CRITICS

1. Chris Kahlenborn and Ann Moell, "What a Woman Should Know about Contraceptives" (Dayton, Ohio: One More Soul).

2. Janet Smith, "Natural Law and Sexual Ethics," p. 12, www.goodmorals.org.

3. *Humanae Vitae*, no. 17.

4. Bishop Victor Galeone, "Marriage: A Communion of Life and Love," 2003 pastoral letter for the diocese of St. Augustine, no. 10, www.omsoul.com.

5. See "The Sound of Wedding Bells May Make the Tax Man Smile," www.savewealth.com.

CHAPTER SIX: TRAINING OUR HEARTS IN TRUTH

1. www.nashvillecathedral.com.

2. www.saintgianna.org.

3. Josemaría Escrivá, *The Way* (Manila: Sinag-Tala, 1982), no. 19, p. 6.

4. Escrivá, no. 179, p. 59.

5. Tim Drake, "Couples Ask: What's Wrong With In-vitro Fertilization?" *National Catholic Register*, www.catholiceducation.org.

6. Congregation for the Doctrine of the Faith, *Donum Vitae*, Instruction on Respect for Human Life, February 22, 1987, no. 8, www.vatican.va.

7. Pope Paul VI Institute, 6901 Mercy Rd., Omaha, NE 68106, (402) 390-6600, www.popepaulvi.com.

8. See Appendix, "Ministering to Moms," in Kimberly Hahn, *Life-Giving Love: Embracing God's Beautiful Design for Marriage* (Cincinnati: Servant, 2002), pp. 349–355.

PART THREE: SHE MAKES LINEN GARMENTS AND SELLS THEM

CHAPTER SEVEN: FACING THE FINANCIAL FUTURE WITHOUT FEAR

1. *Letter to Families*, no. 17.

2. Brenda Hunter, *Home by Choice: Understanding the Enduring*

Effects of a Mother's Love (Sisters, Oreg.: Multnomah, 1991), p. 65.

3. www.ewtn.com.
4. See Patricia Fripp, "The Rule of Three," www.fripp.com.
5. Alice von Hildebrand, *Women at Work* (New Rochelle, N.Y.: Scepter, 1985), p. 10, quoting G.K. Chesterton, *What's Wrong with the World?* (Mineola, N.Y.: Dover, 2007), p. 153.
6. Pope John Paul II, Address on Breastfeeding, May 12, 1995, no. 2, citing Pope Pius XII, Allocution to Mothers, October 26, 1941, www.catholic-forum.com.
7. Kimberly Hahn, *Chosen and Cherished: Biblical Wisdom for Your Marriage* (Cincinnati: Servant, 2002), p. 118.

CHAPTER EIGHT: ECONOMICS OF A STAY-AT-HOME MOM

1. Search the Internet for "Tightwad Christmas." Also see www. bensbargains.net, www.dealsofamerica.com, and www.slickdeals.net.
2. An online mortgage calculator is available at www.bankrate.com.

CHAPTER NINE: MARY, MODEL FOR MOTHERS

1. *Evangelium Vitae*, no. 102.

PART FOUR: HER HUSBAND IS KNOWN IN THE GATES

CHAPTER TEN: THE PERFECT PARENT

1. Holly Pierlot, *A Mother's Rule of Life: How to Bring Order to Your Home and Peace to Your Soul* (Manchester, N.H.: Sophia Institute, 2004), p. 109.
2. Based on C.G. Jung's *Psychological Types* (1921). Dr. Katharine Cook Briggs and her daughter, Dr. Isabel Briggs Myers, developed the Myers-Briggs Type Indicator, an instrument for determining a person's personality profile. For more information see the Myers and Briggs Foundation Web site, www.myersbriggs.org.
3. See Art and Laraine Bennett's *The Temperament God Gave You: The Classic Key to Knowing Yourself, Getting Along with Others, and Growing Closer to the Lord*; Conrad Hock, "The Four Temperaments," www.angelicum.net.

4. See Gary Chapman and Ross Campbell, *The Five Love Languages of Children* (Chicago: Northfield, 1997).

5. James F. McElhone, *Particular Examen: How to Root Out Hidden Faults* (Notre Dame, Ind.: Ave Maria, 1953), p. 96.

6. McElhone, pp. 94–95.

CHAPTER ELEVEN: BRINGING UP CHILDREN WITH DISCIPLINE AND INSTRUCTION

1. Elisabeth Elliot, *The Shaping of a Christian Family—How My Parents Nurtured My Faith* (Grand Rapids: Revell, 2005), p. 10.

PART FIVE: SHE OPENS HER MOUTH WITH WISDOM

CHAPTER TWELVE: MAKING A HOME FOR THE WORD

1. *Familiaris Consortio,* no. 36.

2. *Letter to Families,* no. 16.

3. Pope John Paul II, *Catechesi Tradendae,* Apostolic Exhortation on Catechesis, October 16, 1979, no. 68, www.vatican.va.

4. *Letter to Families,* no. 10.

5. *Catechesi Tradendae,* no. 27.

CHAPTER THIRTEEN: LIVING WITNESSES: SHARING THE FAITH IN OUR FAMILY

1. *Familiaris Consortio,* no. 60.

2. See my chapter in *Catholic for a Reason 2: Scripture and the Mystery of the Mary, Mother of God* for specific suggestions for praying this way.

3. See www.childrenofhope.org.

4. See www.faithandfamilylive.com.

5. See www.holyheroes.com.

6. See www.catholictradition.org for the specific liturgy.

7. See www.fisheaters.com for more information.

PART SIX: THE TEACHING OF KINDNESS IS ON HER TONGUE

CHAPTER FOURTEEN: SCULPTING A LIFE THROUGH EDUCATION AT HOME

1. Edith Schaeffer, *The Hidden Art of Homemaking* (Wheaton, Ill.: Tyndale House, 1986), p. 154.
2. Pope Pius XII, "Guiding Christ's Little Ones," in Vincent A. Yzermans, ed., *The Major Addresses of Pope Pius XII, Volume I: Selected Addresses* (St. Paul: North Central, 1961), p. 42.
3. *Letter to Families,* no. 16.
4. *Letter to Families,* no. 16.
5. *Letter to Families,* no. 17.
6. For more information about homeschooling, please see the book I coauthored with Mary Hasson, *Catholic Education: Homeward Bound* (Ft. Collins, Colo.: Ignatius, 1996).
7. www.littleflowersgirlsclub.blogspot.com.
8. See www.k4j.org.
9. See www.challengeclubs.com.
10. See www.conquestclubs.com.
11. *Familiaris Consortio,* no. 37.

CHAPTER FIFTEEN: TRAINING IN PRACTICAL LIFE SKILLS

1. Here are some of the suggestions from Edith Schaeffer's *The Hidden Art of Homemaking:* Beatrix Potter's *Peter Rabbit,* A.A. Milne's *Winnie the Pooh,* Olive A. Wadsworth's *Over in the Meadow,* Lewis Carroll's *Alice in Wonderland,* T. Cicely M. Barker's *Flower Fairies,* Dick Bruna's books, nursery rhymes, *The Borrowers* series, *Heidi,* Laura Ingalls Wilder's series, *Little Women, Little Men,* Kate S. Eredy's *The Chestery Oak* and *The Good Master,* Joseph Lincoln's stories, Gene Stratton Porter's books, Paul Gallico's children's fairy stories and *Mrs. Harris Goes to Paris, Three Men in a Boat,* Charles Dickens's novels, *Stuart Little, Manx Mouse,* Helen McGinnis's spy stories, Opal Wheeler's stories, Patricia St. John's stories, *Sunshine Country* by Christina Roy, C.S. Lewis's *Narnia* series.
2. Schaeffer, pp. 175–176.

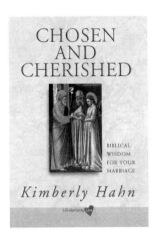

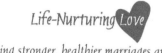

Life-Nurturing Love

building stronger, healthier marriages and families

Graced and Gifted
Biblical Wisdom for the Homemaker's Heart

Volume two in the *Life-Nurturing Love* series will help you create a home that will be a place of beauty and peace where the needs of your loved ones are met. Applying Sacred Scripture, Church teaching, and pastoral wisdom, Hahn helps you explore:

- Time management
- The art of homemaking, from creating a pleasant environment to clutter management
- Food preparation; making meals a time of communion
- Cultivating a garden
- The importance of housework

Book: ISBN 978-0-86716-891-4 | $14.99

Book and 3-DVD set: ISBN 978-0-86716-901-0 | $59.99

Available at www.ServantBooks.org.

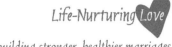

ABOUT THE AUTHOR

KIMBERLY HAHN is the author of *Chosen and Cherished: Biblical Wisdom for Your Marriage, Graced and Gifted: Biblical Wisdom for the Homemaker's Heart, Life-Giving Love: Embracing God's Beautiful Design for Marriage* and coauthor, with her husband Scott Hahn, of *Rome Sweet Home: Our Journey to Catholicism.* She is the mother of six children and is a frequent conference speaker on topics related to marriage and family life.